High Beginners ESL Lesson Plans Book 1

A Conversational Approach

Student Reader
Student Workbook
Teacher Guide

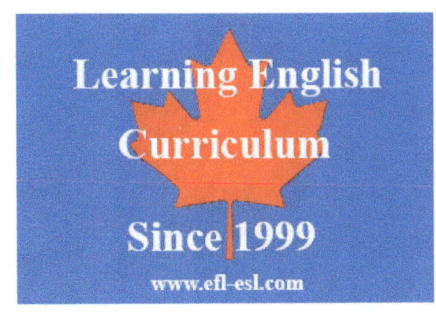

Daisy A. Stocker B.Ed., M.Ed.
George A Stocker D.D.S.

ESL TEEN-ADULT CURRICULUM

High Beginners Part 1

An Interactive Structured Approach to Learning English

This Series Includes a Student Reader, Student Workbook and a Teacher's Guide.

The Students Will Experience Conversation, Grammar, Interactive Activities, Competitive Games, Writing and Speaking in Large and Small Groups.

Learning English Curriculum
Victoria, B.C. Canada
E-mail: **info@efl-esl.com**

Learning English Curriculum

Copyright © 2023 ALL RIGHTS RESERVED.

You are permitted to print or photocopy as many copies as you need for your school. Online distribution is not permitted.

Re-Sales is not permitted.

Notice: Learning English Curriculum makes every reasonable effort to obtain from reliable sources accurate, complete, and timely information about the tests covered in this book. Nevertheless, changes can be made in the tests or the administration of the tests at any time and Learning English Curriculum makes no representation or warranty, either expressed or implied as to the accuracy, timeliness, or completeness of the information contained in this book. Learning English Curriculum make no representations or warranties of any kind, express or implied, about the completeness, accuracy, reliability, suitability or availability with respect to the information contained in this document for any purpose. Any reliance you place on such information is therefore strictly at your own risk.

The author(s) shall not be liable for any loss incurred as a consequence of the use and application, directly or indirectly, of any information presented in this work. Sold with the understanding, the author is not engaged in rendering professional services or advice. If advice or expert assistance is required, the services of a competent professional should be sought.

Published by:
Learning English Curriculum

ISBN 9781772454178

Visit us on the Web at
https://www.efl-esl.com

About Learning English Curriculum Ltd.

Learning English Curriculum began in Czechoslovakia in 1990. Shortly after the Velvet Revolution that freed the country of Communism. The authors began writing these lessons as they taught English to their Czech Students at the English Centre in Karlovy Vary. The students played a vital role in the development of this series. The authors consulted with them by having them complete student surveys wherein they rated the extensive variety of activities and lessons that they had participated in. Discussion of the results followed and any item that was rated below 8, on a scale of 1 to 10, was discarded. Thus, Learning English Curriculum evolved through consultation with our English second language students.

Since 20095 thousands of people around the world have visited our web sites. At this time purchases of our Teen-Adult Curriculum, Children's Curriculum, Children's Storybooks and our listening programs have been made from more than 100 countries.

At Learning English Curriculum, we have a suggestion regarding the printing of our books in an economical and environmentally friendly way. It is our experience that when students begin something new there are always those that, for a number of reasons, don't continue. In order to cut expenses and avoid wasting paper, we suggest that you begin the classes by providing only the first lessons of the printed book. These small things do make a difference.

Customization of your covers

You may be interested in the customization of your covers. (White Label Services
This personalizes your textbooks and makes them a visible part of your school's curriculum. For this service contact us at: info@efl-esl.com

Members of our team with professional degrees have combined years of teaching experience and editing to produce these teaching materials.

Team Members for this publication:
Editors:
Daisy A. Stocker B.Ed., .Ed.
Dr. George A. Stocker D.D.S.

Contributor:
Brian Stocker MA

CONTENTS   HIGH BEGINNERS BOOK 1   LESSONS 1 – 20

This English second language curriculum provided in our Learning English Curriculum Series includes four Modules. Each Book has 20 lessons in Part 1 and 20 in Part 2. The new concepts are incrementally introduced. Each lesson is contained in three books for each Part of each Book: Student Reader, Student Workbook and Teacher's Guide. The Student Reader can be used a number of times as the students aren't required to write in it.

This Table of Contents includes exercises and activities in the Student Reader, Workbook and Teacher's Guide. It also lists the new concepts, oral activities, written exercises and large and small group activities. Answers are included for all questions and discussions. Unit and final tests are provided.

High Beginners Book 1

	Student	Workbook	Guide
Lesson 1	1	1	1

Vocabulary
Role-play
Small group question and answer activity
Word order
Word Bingo
Oral question review of Student Reader Part 1
Oral questions

	Student	Workbook	Guide
Lesson 2		3	5

Vocabulary
Listening and reading paragraphs orally Use of "in" and "on" with time
Small group question and answer activity
Writing answers in sentences
Large group activity
Team activity
Oral questions

	Student	Workbook	Guide
Lesson 3	5	5	9

      Vocabulary
      Tag questions
    Small group question and answer activity
     Using "do" in a tag question
      Word order
      Team activity
      Oral questions

	Student	Workbook	Guide
Lesson 4	7	7	12

      Vocabulary
    Using "this, that, these, those"
      Tag questions
   Recording information from role-cards
      Oral questions

	Student	Workbook	Guide
Lesson 4			14-15

TEST 1

	Student	Workbook	Guide
Lesson 5	8	9	16

      Vocabulary
     Comparative distances
    Small group question and answer activity
   Recording information in the large
    group Writing answers in sentences
      Word Bingo
      Oral questions

	Student	Workbook	Guide
Lesson 6	10	12	18

      Vocabulary
   Paragraph listening and reading orally
    Small group question and answer activity
      The seasons
      Role-play
     Comparative adjectives
      Partner activity
     Completing role-play
      Oral questions

	Student	Workbook	Guide
Lesson 7	13	14	20

Vocabulary
Using comparatives
Role-play
Small group question and answer activity
Small group decision making Answering in sentences
Comparative distances partner activity
Oral questions
Team activity

	Student	Workbook	Guide
Lesson 8	15	16	23

Vocabulary
Department store activity
Review of comparatives
Written answers in sentences
Word Bingo
Oral questions

	Student	Workbook	Guide
Lesson 8 TEST 2			25-26

	Student	Workbook	Guide
Lesson 9	16	19	27

Vocabulary
Paragraph listening and reading orally
Role-play
Small group question and answer activity
Writing sentence answers
Writing comparative sentences
Oral questions

	Student	Workbook	Guide
Lesson 10	18	21	29

Vocabulary
Order of adjectives
Sentence word order using adjectives
Using "a" and "the"
Partner activity using adjectives Writing descriptions using adjectives Writing questions
Oral questions

	Student	Workbook	Guide
Lesson 11	20	24	30

Vocabulary
Adverbs ending in "ly"
Small group question and answer activity
Using "well"
Using adverbs in sentences
Word Bingo
Oral questions

	Student	Workbook	Guide
Lesson 12	21	27	32

Vocabulary
Asking questions in a small group Small group question and answer activity
Adverb review
Word order
Team activity

	Student	Workbook	Guide
Lesson 12 TEST 3			34-35

	Student	Workbook	Guide
Lesson 13	22	29	36

Vocabulary
Frequency adverbs
Small group question and answer activity
Role-play
Using "likely" and "probably"
Writing sentences with frequency adverbs Word Bingo
Oral Questions

	Student	Workbook	Guide
Lesson 14	25	32	39

Vocabulary
Using "ever"
Small group question and answer activity
Small group questions using "ever"
Picture exercise using "ever" Frequency adverb review exercise
Oral questions

		Student	Workbook	Guide
Lesson 15		27	34	41

Vocabulary
Paragraph listening and reading orally Using adverbs with "to be"
Small group question and answer activity
Review of "likely" and "probably"
Writing questions
Word order
Team activity
Oral questions

		Student	Workbook	Guide
Lesson 16		29	36	44

Vocabulary
Paragraph listening and reading orally Whole class activity: Brainstorming ideas Small group question and answer activity Using new vocabulary to complete paragraphs
Completing a role-play
Tag questions
Oral questions

		Student	Workbook	Guide
Lesson 16	**TEST 4**			47

		Student	Workbook	Guide
Lesson 17		31	38	48

Vocabulary
Using "would"
Contractions with "would"
Ordering in a restaurant
Role-plays
Small group question and answer activity
Written exercises using "would"
Team activity
Oral questions

		Student	Workbook	Guide
Lesson 18		34	40	51

Vocabulary
Phrases using words followed by prepositions
Paragraph listening and reading orally Role-play
Small group question and answer activity
Partner activity
Using prepositions
Whole class activity
Oral questions

		Student	Workbook	Guide
Lesson 19		36	42	55

Vocabulary
Using "have got"
Contractions with "have"
Small group question and answer activities
Negative of "have got"
Team activity
Oral questions

		Student	Workbook	Guide
Lesson 20	Review	39	44	59

Role-play
Small group question and answer activities
Comparative distances
Word order
Prepositions
Tag questions
Oral questions

		Student	Workbook	Guide
Lesson 20	FINAL TEST 5			61

Printing this Document

Student Reader - Pages 11 - 52
Student Workbook - Pages 53 - 97
Teacher Guide - Pages 98 - 162

HIGH BEGINNERS ESL LESSON PLANS BOOK 1

STUDENT READER

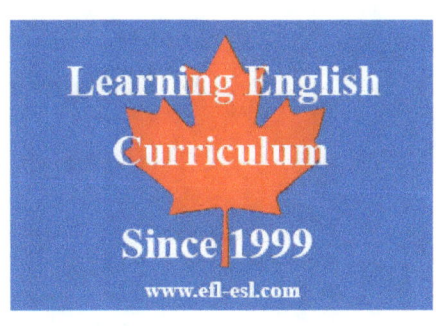

Daisy A. Stocker B.Ed., M.Ed.
George A Stocker D.D.S.

Lesson 1

Oral Questions Teacher Guide

VOCABULARY:	legs			start (to)
time-off	love (to)	note (to)	subject	object
auxiliary verb	move (to)	the best	preposition	think (to)
remember (to)	return (to)	travel (to)	leave (to)	hospital

ACTIVITY 1: Listen to your teacher read what Silvia and Ronald say. Then role-play their dialogue.

Silvia and Ronald are learning to speak English at School this year.

Ronald: Are you working on Friday night Silvia?

Silvia: No, I have some time-off.

Ronald: Can we go to the movies?

Silvia: I can't.

Ronald: Can we go on Saturday night?

Silvia: Yes, that's the best.

Ronald: We can talk about it tomorrow. **Silvia:** Thanks.

https://tinyurl.com/48uvja5p

ACTIVITY 2: Divide into small groups. Ask and answer the questions and then look in the box to check your answer.

1. Where are Silvia and Ronald?
2. Does Silvia have some time-off on Friday night?
3. What does Ronald want to do?
4. Can Silvia go to the movies on Friday night?
5. What is the best time for Silvia to go to the movies?
6. What are they going to do tomorrow?
7. Do you think they will go to the movies on Saturday night?

1. They are at English School.
2. Yes, she does. Yes, she has some time-off.
3. He wants to go to the movies.
4. No, she can't. No, she can't go on Friday night.
5. Saturday is the best.
6. They are going to talk about it.
7. I think they will go to the movies. I don't think they will go to the movies.

EXERCISES 1 AND 2 – WORKBOOK PAGE 1

Student Reader

Lesson 1 Continued

SENTENCE WORD ORDER

They are playing basketball

QUESTION WORD ORDER

What are they playing?

SENTENCE WORD ORDER:

Ruth and Nancy	are playing	basketball	at	school	tonight.
SUBJECT	VERB	OBJECT	PREPOSITION	WHERE	WHEN

QUESTION WORD ORDER

Are	they	playing	basketball	at	school	tonight?
AUXILIARY VERB	SUBJECT	MAIN VERB	OBJECT	PREPOSITION	WHERE	WHEN

ACTIVITY 3: Divide into groups. Read the answer, make the question and check the box. Note the underlined words for the answers and the questions.

1. I can't go out on Friday night.
2. There is a good movie in town.
3. I am working on Friday night.
4. They are going hiking on Saturday.
5. There are many students at the school.
6. He was at the theater.

1. Can you go out on Friday night?
2. Is there a good movie in town?
3. Are you working on Friday night?
4. Are they going hiking on Saturday?
5. Are there many students at the school?
6. Was he at the theater?

ACTIVITY 4   WORKBOOK PAGE 2

Lesson 2

VOCABULARY:
fashion show	born (to be)	younger than	check (to)
cousin	department store	older than	wife
airport	arrive (to)	children	pick up (to)
			relative

ACTIVITY 1: Listen to the audio your teacher read the passage. . Then take turns reading the sentences orally.

Craig, Jessica, Ruth and Raymond are going to visit Craig's brother, Jim, his wife Janet, and their two children Pam and Brian. They live in Canada. Pam and Brian are Ruth and Raymond's cousins.

Craig and his family are going to arrive in Vancouver on Saturday two days from now. They will travel from Melbourne to Sydney by bus and then go by plane to Vancouver, Canada. They are going to arrive at the airport at 10:00 AM*. The two families last saw each other five years ago.

Jim does not work on Saturdays, so Jim, Janet, Pam and Brian will all go to the airport by car to pick up their relatives. Brian is three months younger than Raymond, and Pam is two months older than Ruth. Brian has tickets for a soccer game, and the girls are going to go to a fashion show at one of the department stores.

https://tinyurl.com/2s3mrecd

ACTIVITY 2: Divide into small groups. Ask and answer these questions. Then check your answers.

1. How will Ruth and Raymond travel to Canada?
2. When did they last see their cousins?
3. Does Jim work on Saturdays?
4. Are the boys going to go to a fashion show?

1. They will travel by bus and plane.
2. They last saw their cousins five years ago.
3. No, he doesn't work on Saturdays.
4. No, the boys aren't going to go to a fashion show.

REVIEW: * 10 AM = ten o'clock in the morning.   10 PM = ten o'clock in the evening.

THE USE OF IN AND <u>ON</u> WITH TIME

Raymond was born in May.

MAY ?

"In" means sometime in May.
He was born in May.

Raymond was born on May 25th.
Raymond was born on the 25th of May.

MAY 25th

"On" means a specific day.
He was born on the 25th of May

EXERCISE 1 – WORKBOOK PAGE 3

Lesson 2 Continued

Oral Questions Teacher Guide

ACTIVITY 3: Present and past progressive tenses review.
Ask each other these questions. Answer in sentences.

1. Were you studying English last night?
2. Is your friend wearing blue jeans today?
3. Were you eating breakfast at 8:00 yesterday?
4. Were you drinking coffee at 10:30 today?
5. Were you watching a fashion show last week?
6. Were you reading a book this morning?
7. Was your friend traveling by plane last year?
8. Was your aunt living here last year?
9. Is your uncle visiting you today?
10. Is your cousin working in a department store?
11. Were you picking up your friends last night?
12. Were your relatives living nearby last year?

1. Yes, I was studying English last night. No, I wasn't studying English last night.
2. Yes, my friend is wearing blue jeans today. No, my friend isn't wearing blue jeans today.
3. Yes, I was eating breakfast at 8:00 yesterday. No, I wasn't eating breakfast at 8:00 yesterday.
4. Yes, I was drinking coffee at 10:30 today. No, I wasn't drinking coffee at 10:30 today.
5. Yes, I was watching a fashion show last week. No, I wasn't watching a fashion show last week.
6. Yes, I was reading a book this morning. No, I wasn't reading a book this morning.
7. Yes, my friend was traveling by plane last year. No, my friend wasn't traveling by plane last…
8. Yes, my aunt was living here last year. No, my aunt wasn't living here last…
9. Yes, my uncle is visiting me today. No, my uncle isn't visiting me today.
10. Yes, my cousin is working in a department store. No, my cousin isn't working in a department…
11. Yes, I was picking up my friends last night. No, I wasn't picking up my friends last night.
12. Yes, my relatives were living nearby last year. No, my relatives weren't living nearby last year.

ACTIVITIES 4 AND 5 – WORKBOOK PAGE 4 ACTIVITY 6 – GUIDE PAGES 7,8

Student Reader

Lesson 3

VOCABULARY:
add (to)	grow (to)	summer	end (to)
be able (to)	people	expect (to)	flower
statement	actor		

TAG QUESTIONS
A tag question is a question added to the end of a sentence.
Speakers use tag questions to make sure their information is correct.

ACTIVITY 1 — Divide into Group 1 and Group 2. Listen to your teacher read each example. Then Group 1 role-play Student 1 and Group 2 role-play Student 2.

to be: singular
Student 1: Marietta **is** here, **isn't** she?
Student 2: Yes, she **is**.

to be: plural
Student 1: Silvia and Ronald **are** here, **aren't** they?
Student 2: Yes, they **are**.

to have:
Student 1: You **have** a motorcycle, **haven't** you?
Student 2: Yes, I **have**.

can (to be able):
Student 1: Ken **can't** play ball, **can** he?
Student 2: No, he **can't**.

TWO SPECIAL NOTES: Verb – to be: **I'm** here, **aren't** I?

The tenses are the same for the sentence, question and answer.

EXAMPLE: He **was** at school, **wasn't** he?   She **won't** come, **will** she?
Yes, he **was**.   No, she **won't**.

EXERCISE 1: – WORKBOOK PAGE 5

Student Reader

Lesson 3 Continued

ACTIVITY 2: Divide into small groups. Ask and answer the questions.
Then look in the box to check your answer.
NOTE: The person asking the question is making sure that they understand the other person.

1. You're coming to class tomorrow, aren't you?
2. You can make a good supper, can't you?
3. You have a dog at home, haven't you?
4. Your friend is from New York, isn't he?
5. You aren't Canadian, are you?
6. You weren't here yesterday, were you?
7. You can speak English, can't you?
8. You are a student, aren't you?
9. This is English class, isn't it?
10. We aren't Russian, are we?
11. There are twelve people in this class, aren't there?
12. It isn't raining, is it?

1. Yes, I am.
   No, I'm not.
2. Yes, I can.
   No, I can't.
3. Yes, I have.
   No, I haven't.
4. Yes, he is.
   No, he isn't.
5. No, I'm not
   Yes, I am.
6. No, I wasn't
   Yes, I was.
7. Yes, I can.
   No, I can't.
8. Yes, I am
   No, I'm not.
9. Yes, it is.
10. No, we're not.
    Yes, we are.
11. Yes, there are.
    No, there aren't.
12. No, it isn't.
    Yes, it is.

USING DO IN A TAG QUESTION
We often use "do" when asking a tag question. See page 5 of the workbook for exceptions.

EXAMPLES: They **don't** live here, **do** they?   No, they **don't**.

He **doesn't** play soccer, **does** he?   No, he **doesn't**.

She **likes** to swim, **doesn't** she?   Yes, she **does**.

You **played** basketball yesterday, **didn't** you?   Yes, I **did**.

ACTIVITY 3: Work with your teacher to ask these tag questions, give the answers using "do".

You walked to class, _____ ___ ? Yes, I ____.   We come from Canada, _____ __ ? Yes, we ___

We study English, _____ ___ ? Yes, we ___.   We eat at noon, _____ ___ ?   Yes. we ____.

Oral Questions Teacher Guide

EXERCISE 2 – WORKBOOK PAGE 5
ACTIVITY 4 – WORKBOOK PAGE 6
EXERCISE 3 – WORKBOOK PAGE 6
ACTIVITY 4 – GUIDE PAGES 10, 11

Student Reader

Lesson 4 REVIEW

Listen to your teacher and repeat these words.

VOCABULARY:

far	near	greater
the nearest	elephant	farther
mean (to)	distance	those
boat	away	

THIS / THAT (singular)

These birds are near us.
This big car is near us.
This and **these** mean nearby.

THESE / THOSE (plural)

That small car is far away.
Those birds are farther away.
That and **those** mean a greater distance.

EXERCISES 1 AND 2 – WORKBOOK PAGE 7
EXERCISE 3 – WORKBOOK PAGES 7, 8
EXERCISE 4 – WORKBOOK PAGE 8
ACTIVITY 1 – WORKBOOK PAGE 8 AND PAGE 12 OF GUIDE

This man is going to have a big problem.

Those girls are dancing.

Student Reader

Lesson 5

VOCABULARY:	Spelling – "center" American		"centre" - British
close to	the biggest	far from	point (to)
closer to	bigger than	farther from	than
the closest	nearer to	the farthest	kilometer
as close to ____ as	the nearest	as far from ____ as	old
young	as near to ____ as	the same distance from	older than

COMPARATIVE DISTANCES

ACTIVITY 1: Listen to your teacher read each sentence.
Point to the English School and then point to the correct house.

Mary's house is far from the English School.
Joe's house is farther from the English School than Mary's.
Ann's house is the farthest from the English School.
Bill's house is closer to the English School than Mary's house.
Pat's house is the closest to the English School.
Jean's house is the same distance from the English School as Bill's house.

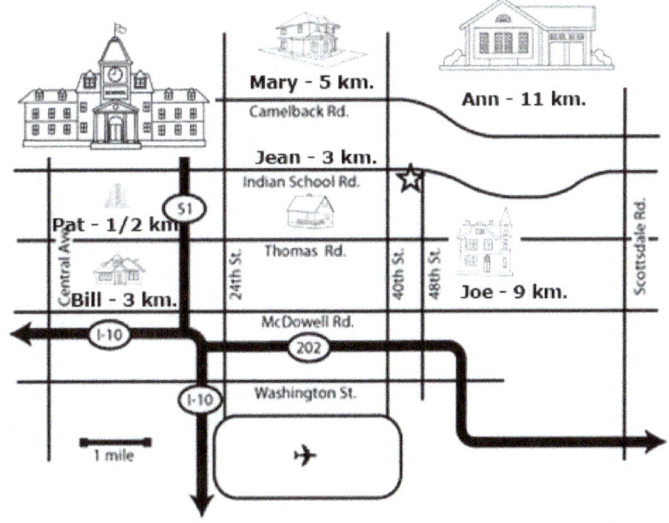

ACTIVITY 2: Divide into small groups.
Ask and answer the questions. Check your answers.

1. Does Mary live farther from the English School than Bill?
2. Who lives the farthest from the English School?
3. Who lives the closest to the English School?
4. Who lives the same distance from the English School as Jean?
5. Does Joe live as far from the English School as Ann?

1. Yes, she lives farther from the English School than Bill.
2. Ann lives the farthest from the English School.
3. Pat lives the closest to the English School.
4. Bill lives the same distance from the English School as Jean.
5. No, Joe doesn't live as far from the English School as Ann.

ACTIVITY 3 – WORKBOOK PAGE 9
EXERCISE 1 – WORKBOOK PAGE 9
EXERCISE 2 – WORKBOOK PAGE 10
ACTIVITY 4 – WORKBOOK PAGE 11
TEST 1 – GUIDE PAGES 14 AND 15

Oral Questions Teacher Guide

Student Reader

Lesson 6

VOCABULARY:

interested (in)	birthday	more than	better
department store	the most	international	season
north	sports	weather	winter
etcetera = etc.	sun	part	world

ACTIVITY 1:

Listen to the audio your teacher read the passage. . Then take turns reading the sentences.

Raymond and Ruth are from Melbourne, Australia. They are visiting their Canadian cousins Brian and Pam. They find many interesting things to do with their cousins.

Ruth loves clothes and she loves her long hair. She wants to look at the clothes in the department stores. Pam likes clothes, too, but she is more interested in sports.

Ruth got some new clothes for her birthday. She was born on the twenty-fifth of November. Pam's birthday is on January twenty-eighth. She is two months younger than Ruth.

https://tinyurl.com/4797c9wf

ACTIVITY 2:

Ask and answer the questions. Then check your answers.

1. Where do Pam and Brian live?
2. What is Ruth interested in?
3. What is Pam interested in?
4. What does Ruth like to do?
5. Pam is younger than Ruth, isn't she?
6. Ruth got some new clothes for her birthday, didn't she?
7. When is Pam's birthday?

1. They live in Canada.
2. She is interested in clothes.
3. Pam is interested in sports.
4. She likes to look at clothes in the department stores.
5. Yes, she is.
6. Yes, she did.
7. Pam's birthday is on January twenty-eighth.

Student Reader

Lesson 6 Continued

ACTIVITY 3: Ask and answer the questions. Then check your answers.

Brian and Raymond are interested in soccer. They like to watch the international games. Brian says India has the strongest teams. Raymond thinks the Canadians are the best players. They are going to go to a soccer game on Friday. A team from India will be playing the Canadians. Kabir is the star India player.

1. What are Brian and Raymond interested in?

2. What games do they like to watch?

3. What does Raymond think?

4. What does Brian say about the Indians teams?

5. When are they going to go to a soccer game?

https://tinyurl.com/mup7r389

1. They are interested in soccer.
2. They like to watch the International games.
3. Raymond thinks the Canadians are the best players.
4. Brian says the Indians have the strongest teams.
5. They're going to go on Friday.

EXERCISE 1 – WORKBOOK PAGE 12

REFERENCE INFORMATION: THE SEASONS

Some places have four seasons each year while others have a wet season and a dry season. Canada has four seasons.

Spring: March 21st to June 21st – it is getting warmer.

Summer: June 21st to September 21st – it is the warmest time of year.

Fall (Autumn) September 21st to December 21st – it is getting colder.

Winter: December 21st to March 21st – it is the coldest time of year.

EXERCISE 1 - PAGE 12 WORKBOOK

Lesson 6 Continued

ACTIVITY 4: ORAL QUESTIONS   Teacher Guide

Listen to your the audio and your teacher read the dialogue. Then role-play it in small groups.

https://tinyurl.com/3p4nm3xd

Narrator: Raymond, Ruth, Brian and Pam are talking about a new Canadian department store that has opened in Brian and Pam's city.

Raymond: I hear you have a new department store here.

Brian: Yes, I went to their sports department yesterday.

Pam: I was there, too.

Pam: Our stores have clothes for cold weather, hot rainy weather and beautiful warm weather.

Brian: They have mountain bikes, too.

Pam: Some places in Canada are very hot in the summer.

Raymond: Our winters aren't as cold as yours are.

Pam: No, but our cold winters give us the best sports.

Brian: I love winter sports!

ACTIVITY 5   **WORKBOOK PAGE 12**

EXERCISES 2 AND 3 – WORKBOOK PAGE 13

Student Reader   11

Lesson 6 Continued

COMPARATIVE ADJECTIVES (REFERENCE INFORMATION)

Most comparative adjectives are regular. Here are some of the common ones:

short	shorter	the shortest
tall	taller	the tallest
long	longer	the longest
wide	wider	the widest
old	older	the oldest
young	younger	the youngest
late	later	the latest
fast	faster	the fastest
slow	slower	the slowest
cheap	cheaper	the cheapest
narrow	narrower	the narrowest
near	nearer	the nearest
light	lighter	the lightest
cold	colder	the coldest
great	greater	the greatest
few	fewer	the fewest

If the one-syllabic adjective ends with a single consonant, we double the final consonant.

fat	fatter	the fattest
thin	thinner	the thinnest
sad	sadder	the saddest
mad	madder	the maddest
hot	hotter	the hottest

If an adjective ends with a "y", change the "y" to "i" before adding the ending:

pretty	prettier	the prettiest
dry	drier	the driest
hungry	hungrier	the hungriest
heavy	heavier	the heaviest
early	earlier	the earliest

There are a few irregular comparative adjectives:

good	better	the best
some	more	the most
bad	worse	the worst
less	lesser	the least
far	farther	the farthest

Student Reader

Lesson 7

VOCABULARY:	expensive	heavy	a few	fast
tall	early	light	fewer	faster
short	cheap	the least	the fewest	the fastest
wide	slow	but	on sale	a lot of
narrow				

ACTIVITY 1 Listen to the audio and your teacher read each passages

Then take turns reading the sentences and answer the question orally

Ruth and Pam went to a big store to look at clothes.
They saw many clothes that were cheap.
They were not good clothes.
1. Were these clothes expensive?

Next, they went to a better store, a smaller store.
There weren't as many clothes and they were more expensive.
2. Was this smaller store better than the big one?

Later they went to the best dress store. It was the smallest store.
It had the fewest clothes and they were the most expensive.
Ruth said that her friend, Sarita in Delhi had an expensive dress like that.

3. Does the smallest store have the most expensive clothes?

The boys didn't want to look at clothes.
They talked about things they were interested in.

Raymond has a bicycle.
He can go very fast.
4. What does Raymond have?

Brian has a motorcycle.
He can go faster than Raymond.
5. Can Brian go faster than Raymond?

Brian's father has a Mercedes sports car.
He can go the fastest.
6. Who can go the fastest?

Oral Questions Teacher Guide
EXERCISE 1 – WORKBOOK PAGE 14

Student Reader

Lesson 7 Continued

ACTIVITY 2: Role-play the dialogue three or four times.

Then answer the questions and check your answers.

PAM: Isn't that small store interesting!

RUTH: It's great but it's too expensive.

PAM: It's too expensive for me too, but I liked their sports clothes.

RUTH: We have stores like that at home.

PAM: Are they in the small towns in your country?

RUTH: There are many different types of stores in our big cities, but there aren't many stores in our small towns.

https://tinyurl.com/2p8jxbz3

ACTIVITY 3: Ask and answer the questions and check your answers.

1. Did the girls like the small store?

2. Was the small store a cheap store or was it very expensive?

3. What kind of clothes did Pam like?

4. Does Ruth have expensive stores in the big city where she lives?

5. ...nds of stores in the big cities?

1. Yes, they liked the small store. They thought it was interesting.
2. It was an expensive store.
3. She liked the sports clothes.
4. Yes, she has expensive stores in the big city where she lives.
5. Yes, there are. Yes, the big cities have many kinds of stores.

ACTIVITY 4: All the girls are to sit in one group and all the boys are to sit in another group.

Talk about the two questions and decide what your group thinks.

GIRLS:

1. Do you find good cheap clothes for sale?

2. What kind of stores do you like the best?

BOYS:

1. What sport do you like the best?

2. Which kind of sports car or motorcycle do you like the best?

Return to the large group and tell the class what your group decided.

EXERCISES 2 AND 3 – WORKBOOK PAGE 15
ACTIVITY 5 – WORKBOOK PAGE 15
ACTIVITY 6 – GUIDE PAGE 22

Student Reader

Lesson 8 REVIEW

VOCABULARY:
money   opposite   worse   equipment
everyone   accessories   the worst

ACTIVITY 1:   You are in a big department store.

It has a:
girl's shoe department

boy's shoe department

girl's clothes department

boy's clothes department

Sports equipment department for everyone:

bicycles and bicycle accessories
car accessories
hiking and mountain climbing equipment

Decide where you will go. Now move about the classroom and ask:
What department will you go to?
When you find another student or students who will go to the same department, sit together and decide what you will buy.

Return to the large group and tell the class what you will buy.

Oral Questions Teacher Guide

EXERCISES 1 AND 2 – WORKBOOK PAGE 16

ACTIVITY 2 – WORKBOOK PAGE 17

ACTIVITY 3 – WORKBOOK PAGE 18

TEST 2 – GUIDE PAGES 25 AND 26

Student Reader   15

Lesson 9

VOCABULARY:

wet	smart	take (to)	cheese	sandwich
stupid	terrible	pickle	paragraph	bathing suit
hate (to)	horse	sorry	beach	the most

ACTIVITY 1:

**Listen to your teacher read each paragraph.
Take turns reading the sentences orally and then answer the questions.**

Ruth, Pam, Raymond and Brian decided to go to the lake.
They took their dog, Toto. Brian thinks that Toto is the stupidest dog.
Pam took some cheese sandwiches and some juice.
They took more sandwiches for the boys than for the girls.
Raymond ate the most, and Pam ate the least.

What does Brian think about Toto?
Who ate the most sandwiches?

When they got too hot, they all went into the water.
Toto got into the water first, and Brian was the last to get wet.
He said that the water was too cold, and that last time the water was warmer.
They all had a good time.
They went home before it got very hot.
   3.   **Who got wet first?**
Who was the last to get wet?

EXERCISE 1 – WORKBOOK PAGE 19

Student Reader

Lesson 9 Continued

ACTIVITY 2: Role-play the dialogue with the whole class. Then divide into groups of four or five and role-play, changing roles.

Narrator: The four cousins are at the lake. Raymond likes tea and Ruth can't eat cheese sandwiches. They talk about finding a place where they can buy something to eat and drink. Ruth and Brian are Canadian. Raymond is Australian and Pam is British

Ruth: Let's have lunch now.

Raymond: What are we going to have?

Pam: We brought cheese and pickle sandwiches and juice.

Raymond: Did you bring some tea, too?

Brian: No, I think it's too hot to drink tea.

Raymond: I always drink tea. We Australians love tea.

Ruth: Are all the sandwiches made with cheese?

Pam: Yes, cheese and pickles.

Brian: Don't you like cheese?

Ruth: No, I'm sorry, I can't eat cheese.

Raymond: I saw a small restaurant nearby. Can we go there?

Ruth: Good idea! We can get what we want there and we'll come back here later.

Brian: I'm hungry. I'll have a cheese sandwich on the way there.

https://tinyurl.com/ynyhp7nc

ACTIVITY 3: Ask and answer these questions. Then check your answers.

1. Where are the cousins?
2. What does Raymond like to drink?
3. What did Pam bring to eat for lunch?
4. What did she bring to drink?
5. Who can't eat cheese?
6. What did Raymond see nearby?
7. How did Brian feel?
8. What did Brian want to have before going to the restaurant?
9. Do you eat sandwiches?

1. They are at the lake.
2. He likes to drink tea.
3. She brought some cheese and pickle sandwiches.
4. She brought some juice.
5. Ruth can't eat cheese.
6. He saw a small restaurant.
7. He felt hungry.
8. He wanted to have a cheese sandwich.
9. Yes, I eat sandwiches. No, I don't eat sandwiches.

Oral Questions Teacher Guide

EXERCISE 2 - WORKBOOK PAGE 19
EXERCISES 3, 4 AND 5 – WORKBOOK PAGE 20

Student Reader

Lesson 10

ACTIVITY 1: Repeat these words after your teacher.

VOCABULARY:

gray	baseball	colorful	little
cotton	baby	alone	huge
stripe	hair	long	black
change (to)	modify (to)	red	green
blue	yellow	purple	

ADJECTIVES

Adjectives describe or modify nouns.
The word *modify* means: *to change a little.*
Adjectives change the meaning of a noun a little.

SENTENCE WORD ORDER USING ADJECTIVES

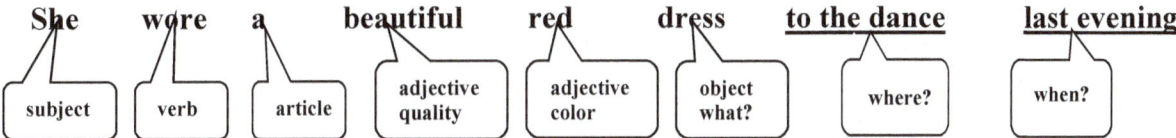

She (subject) wore (verb) a (article) beautiful (adjective quality) red (adjective color) dress (object what?) to the dance (where?) last evening (when?)

ADJECTIVE AND NOUN MODIFIERS

If there is more than one modifier, they should be put into the following order.

ORDER OF ADJECTIVES

number	size	quality	color	pattern	nationality	material	noun as modifier	noun
two	big	cheap	gray	striped	Canadian	cotton	baseball	hats

EXAMPLES:

I have a hat.
I have a baseball hat.
I have two baseball hats.
I have two cotton baseball hats.
I have two gray cotton baseball hats.
I have two new gray cotton baseball hats.
I have two new gray Canadian cotton baseball hats.

EXERCISES 1 AND 2 – WORKBOOK PAGE 21

Student Reader

Lesson 10 Continued

NOTE:

Adjectives aren't singular or plural.

A final "s" **isn't** added to an adjective.

EXAMPLE:

<u>There's</u> a baby elephant.
Those <u>huge</u> <u>gray</u> elephants are standing together.

CONTRACTIONS:

there is = there's

Oral Questions — Teacher Guide

ARTICLES
a   the

Use an article before the adjective if it modifies a <u>singular</u> noun.

EXAMPLE: <u>The</u> baby elephant is standing alone.

ACTIVITY 1: Your teacher will help you to answer these questions.
Look around you as you answer these questions.

1. Who is wearing a big red hat?

2. Is someone wearing a light green shirt?

3. Who is wearing a warm jacket?

4. Who is wearing new blue jeans?

5. Who has old black shoes?

6. Who has a short blue pencil?

7. Is your teacher wearing a long yellow dress?

8. Is it a cold snowy day today?

ACTIVITY 2 – WORKBOOK PAGE 21
EXERCISE 3 – WORKBOOK PAGE 22
ACTIVITY 3 – WORKBOOK PAGE 22
EXERCISE 4 – WORKBOOK PAGE 23
ACTIVITY 4 – WORKBOOK PAGE 23

Student Reader

Lesson 11

ADVERBS

Adverbs modify verbs. They often answer the question "How?"
How does he walk? He walks <u>quickly</u>.

Adverbs are often formed by adding – "ly" to the adjective.
These adverbs usually come after the verb.
He works <u>slowly</u>.

Listen to and repeat these adjectives and adverbs after your teacher.

bad - badly	busy - busily	thin - thinly	glad - gladly
heavy - heavily	hour - hourly	hungry - hungrily	sad - sadly
slow - slowly	month - monthly	nice - nicely	night - nightly
polite - politely	careful - carefully	quick – quickly	loud - loudly

VOCABULARY

careful	aunt	uncle	eye
polite	cross (to)	cut (to)	piece
job	extreme	sun	wash (to)
	gift	bread	because

NOTE: If the adjective ends in a <u>consonant + y</u>, change the <u>y</u> to <u>i</u> and add <u>ly</u>.
busy - bus<u>i</u>ly   heavy - heav<u>i</u>ly   hungry - hungr<u>i</u>ly

Adverbs are often used to modify adjectives.

He is a <u>very</u> old man.   She has <u>extremely</u> long hair.

Oral Questions   Teacher Guide

EXERCISES 1 AND 2 – WORKBOOK PAGE 24
ACTIVITY 1 – WORKBOOK PAGE 24
EXERCISE 3 – WORKBOOK PAGE 25
ACTIVITY 2 – WORKBOOK PAGE 25
ACTIVITY 3 – WORKBOOK PAGE 26

Lesson 12 REVIEW

VOCABULARY

happy – happily	joy – joyfully	quiet – quietly	guy	hundred
less	building	pull (to)	strong	forest
				dress (to)

ACTIVITY 1: Divide into small groups.
Ask these questions adding the name of the person you are talking about.
The person asked answers in a sentence.

EXAMPLE: QUESTION: Does _____ (name of a person in the room) have long brown hair?
ANSWER: Yes, he / she has long brown hair.
No, he / she doesn't have long brown hair.

1. Is _____ wearing new blue jeans?
2. Is _____ wearing long black pants?
3. Does _____ have a red pen in his / her hand?
4. Does _____ have short black hair?
5. Is _____ wearing big round glasses?
6. Is _____ wearing small red shoes?
7. Is _____ wearing a blue cotton hat?
8. Is _____ wearing a long green dress?
9. Are you wearing a small watch?
10. Is our teacher wearing a short red dress?
11. Is _____ wearing an old brown T-shirt?
12. Does _____ have a beautiful new notebook?

ACTIVITY 2 Ask and answer these questions. Then check your answers

1. Is your group talking quietly?

2. Do a lot of guys practice archery?

3. Do you live in a big tall building?

4. Is there a forest near here?

5. Do children play games joyfully?

6. Is one hundred less than two hundred?

7. Do you know the time?

1. Yes, our group is talking quietly.
   No, our group isn't talking quietly.
2. Yes, a lot of guys practice archery.
   No, most guys don't practice archery.
3. Yes, I live in a big tall building.
   No, I don't live in a big tall building.
4. Yes, there's a forest near here.
   No, there isn't a forest near here.
5. Yes, children play games joyfully.
6. Yes, one hundred is less than two hundred.
7. Yes, it's _____.

EXERCISE 1 – WORKBOOK PAGE 27
EXERCISES 2 AND 3 – WORKBOOK PAGE 28

ACTIVITY 3 – GUIDE PAGE 33
TEST 3 – GUIDE PAGES 34 AND 35

Student Reader

Lesson 13

Listen to your teacher and repeat the vocabulary words and the adverbs.

VOCABULARY:

casually	stay up (to)	helicopter	go out (to)	vegetable
together	somewhere	different	concert	fruit

FREQUENCY OR MID SENTENCE ADVERBS:

usually		generally	
occasionally	sometimes	often	just
frequently	mostly	seldom	finally
never	hardly ever		
probably	likely	already	always

REFERENCE INFORMATION

FREQUENCY OR MID SENTENCE ADVERBS

Some adverbs are placed in the middle of a sentence. (mid sentence adverbs)

1) Put mid-sentence adverbs <u>in front of</u> simple present and simple past verbs.
   Anne <u>always comes</u> on time.

2) Exception - Adverbs are placed <u>after</u> the verb <u>to be</u>.
   Anne <u>is always</u> on time.

3) Adverbs are placed <u>between</u> a helping verb and the main verb.
   Anne <u>is always coming</u> on time.

4) In a question, a mid-sentence adverb always comes directly after the subject.
   Does   (she)   (always)   come on time?
          (subject)   (adverb)

COMMON MID-SENTENCE (FREQUENCY) ADVERBS:

never, hardly ever, seldom -	Answer using "no".	No, I seldom walk.
occasionally, sometimes, usually, generally -	Answer using "yes".	Yes, I generally walk.
frequently, mostly, often, always -	Answer using "yes".	Yes, I always walk.
probably, likely -	Answer using "yes".	Yes, I will likely walk.
already -	Answer using "yes".	Yes, he already came.
finally -	Answer using "yes".	Yes, he finally came.
just -	Answer using "yes".	Yes, he just arrived.
ever -	See the use of "ever" on page 25 of this book.	

Student Reader

Lesson 13 Continued

> **1)** Put mid-sentence adverbs <u>in front of</u> simple present and simple past verbs.
> Anne <u>always comes</u> on time.

ACTIVITY 1:   **ASK YOUR PARTNER**
Answer using a mid-sentence adverb from page 22.

EXAMPLE: Do you play volleyball?
Yes, I <u>sometimes</u> play volleyball.   No, I <u>never</u> play volleyball.

Note: Choose your adverbs to express your meaning.
The answers in the box are just possible answers. Yours may be different.

1. Do you eat sandwiches for lunch?
2. Do you buy dresses?
3. Did you go to Calcutta last year?
4. Do you read books?
5. Do you go to department stores?
6. Do you travel by boat?
7. Do you go to fashion shows?
8. Do you swim?
9. Do you drive a motorcycle?
10. Do you come to class by helicopter?
11. Did you eat hamburgers last year?
12. Do you see your relatives on the weekend?

1. Yes, I sometimes eat sandwiches for lunch. / No, I never eat sandwiches for lunch.
2. Yes, I often buy dresses. / No, I never buy dresses.
3. Yes, I frequently went to Calcutta last year. / No, I hardly ever went to Calcutta.
4. Yes, I frequently read books. / No, I never read books.
5. Yes, I often go to department stores. / No, I never go to department stores.
6. Yes, I frequently travel by boat. / No, I never travel by boat.
7. Yes, I often go to fashion shows. / No, I hardly ever go to fashion shows.
8. Yes, I occasionally swim. / No, I hardly ever swim.
9. Yes, I always drive a motorcycle. / No, I never drive a motorcycle.
10. Yes, I frequently come to class by helicopter. / No, I never come to class by helicopter.
11. Yes, I frequently ate hamburgers last year. / No, I seldom ate hamburgers last year.
12. Yes, I usually see my relatives on the weekend. / No, I never see my relatives on the weekend.

Lesson 13 Continued

EXERCISE 1 – WORKBOOK PAGE 29   **Oral Questions   Teacher Guide**

ACTIVITY 2:   NOTE: "**to go out**" means - to go away from where you are.
"**just**" is often used to mean that something happened or will happen within a few minutes.
Listen to your teacher read the dialogue. Then take turns role-playing it for the whole class.
Answer the questions orally.

Carol:	Tom, how are you doing?
Tom:	I'm okay but I'm very tired of working.
Carol:	We're always working.
Tom:	That's right! We hardly ever go out.
Carol:	I'd like to just walk out of here now!
Tom:	Let's go!
Carol:	Let's go somewhere different.
Tom:	Sarah and Peter often go to concerts.
Carol:	Yes, our theaters usually have good concerts.

1. Who was very tired of working?
2. Do Carol and Tom frequently go to concerts?
3. Do they often go out?
4. Do their theaters have good concerts?
5. Do Peter and Sarah go to many concerts?

ACTIVITY 3:   USING <u>LIKELY</u> AND <u>PROBABLY</u> ASK YOUR PARTNER

EXAMPLE: Are you going to see your friend tonight?
Yes, I'll <u>probably</u> see my friend tonight.   No, I won't <u>likely</u> see my friend tonight.

NOTE: We usually use "likely" with the negative.

1. Will you go to the theatre tonight?
2. Are you going to come to class next week?
3. Will you move to Delhi next year?
4. Are you going to take a bus home tonight?
5. Are you going to play basketball tomorrow?
6. Are you going to buy a jacket next year?
7. Are you going to ride a bicycle to class?

1. I will (I'll) likely go to the theater tonight.
   I won't likely go to the theater tonight.
2. Yes, I'm likely going to come to class next week.
   No, I'm not likely going to come to class next week.
3. Yes, I'll likely move to Delhi next year.
   No, I won't likely move to Delhi next year.
4. Yes, I'll probably take a bus home tonight.
   No, I won't likely take a bus home tonight.
5. Yes, I'll probably play basketball tomorrow.
   No, I won't likely play basketball tomorrow.
6. Yes, I'll likely buy a jacket next year.
   No, I won't likely buy a jacket next year.
7. Yes, I'll probably ride a bicycle to class.
   No, I won't likely ride a bicycle to class.

EXERCISE 2 – WORKBOOK PAGE 30
EXERCISE 3 – WORKBOOK PAGE 30
ACTIVITY 4 – WORKBOOK PAGE 31

Student Reader

Lesson 14

VOCABULARY:

dance (to)	agree	sleep in (to)	dragon
favorite	thick	cost (to)	cook (to)
ghost	much	ever	bananas

USING THE ADVERB "EVER".

"Ever" is used <u>only</u> in a negative statement and in a question because it means:
-did something happen even once?

EXAMPLE: Did you <u>ever</u> go to New York?   I <u>didn't ever</u> go to New York.

"Ever" is <u>not used</u> in a positive statement,
except when a supporting adverb goes before it.

EXAMPLE: Do you <u>ever</u> travel by boat?
<u>Yes</u>, I travel by boat.
No, I <u>never</u> travel by boat.   No, I <u>hardly ever</u> travel by boat.

ACTIVITY 1:   **Divide into small groups.**
Ask and answer these questions, then check the answers. Use the correct tense.

EXAMPLE: Do you <u>ever</u> dance?   <u>Yes</u>, I dance.   <u>No</u>, I don't <u>ever</u> dance.

1. Did you ever go to Canada? (no)
2. Do you ever go swimming? (yes)
3. Do you ever buy food in the stores? (yes)
4. Do clothes ever cost too much? (yes)
5. Do you ever stay up late? (no)
6. Did you ever pull in a tug-of-war? (yes)
7. Do you ever agree with your friend? (yes)
8. Did you ever sleep in? (no)
9. Did you ever want to hear a loud concert? (no)

1. No, I didn't ever go to Canada.
   No, I never went to Canada.
2. Yes, I go swimming.
3. Yes, I buy food in the stores.
4. Yes, they cost too much.
5. No, I hardly ever stay up late.
   No, I don't ever stay up late.
   No, I never stay up late.
6. Yes, I pulled in a tug-of-war.
7. Yes, I agree with my friend.
8. No, I didn't ever sleep in.
   No, I never slept in.
9. No, I didn't ever want to hear a loud concert.
   No, I never wanted to hear a loud concert.

EXERCISE 1 – WORKBOOK PAGE 32

Student Reader

Lesson 14 Continued

Oral Questions Teacher Guide

ACTIVITY 2: **USING EVER / NEVER**
Divide into small groups.
Look at each picture. Complete the question orally and ask someone in the group.
The person asked must answer orally in a sentence.

EXAMPLE: Do you ever go hiking? Yes, I go hiking.
No, I don't ever go hiking.
No, I never go hiking.

REMEMBER! Don't use "ever" when the answer is "yes".

Yes, I go hiking.

EXCEPTION: hardly ever   **EXAMPLE:** I <u>hardly ever</u> drink coffee.

Do you ever go to the _____?

Do you ever eat _____?

Do you ever go _____?

Do you ever take a _____

Do you ever read a _____

Do you ever have _____?

Do you ever go _____?

Do you ever drive a _____

Do you ever wear a _____?

EXERCISES 2 AND 3 – WORKBOOK PAGE 33

Student Reader

Lesson 15

VOCABULARY:

handicap	help (to)	alcohol	dark
drug	problem	die (to)	rich
street	unfortunate	world	face (to), faced
cause (to)			

street people (they live on the streets)

https://tinyurl.com/4wb5t8se

ACTIVITY 1:

Listen to your teacher read these paragraphs. Then take turns reading the sentences orally.

The Street People

Sometimes people have bad times. They face bad times when a mother or father dies and there isn't any money. Sometimes people are handicapped. They can't get a job. These people feel very alone. This is often the start of a bigger problem with alcohol or drugs. They think these things will help them, but their problems just get worse. Then they must live on the street because they have no job, no money, no family and no friends.

Victoria is one of the richest cities in Canada. It is known as "The City of Gardens." Everywhere there are beautiful gardens, but if you look carefully in some of the dark corners of the city, you will find these unfortunate people. The beautiful gardens don't help them. The world walks by, and no one sees them.

USING ADVERBS WITH THE VERB "TO BE".

A mid-sentence adverb comes <u>after</u> the verb <u>to be</u>. (am / is / are, was / were)

EXAMPLE: Anne   (is)   (always) on time.
   (verb <u>to be</u>) (adverb)

ACTIVITY 2: Ask and answer the questions orally using any of the mid-sentence adverbs from the list. Then check the possible answers.

sometimes   often   never   seldom   frequently   usually   likely   hardly ever
very   always

1. Are you alone?

2. Is alcohol the cause of many problems?

3. Are you asleep at night?

4. Are drugs from the streets helpful?

5. Are the streets a comfortable place to sleep?

6. Are street people rich?

7. Were the street people in Victoria feeling alone?

1. I am often alone.
2. Yes, alcohol is frequently the cause of many problems.
3. Yes, I'm always asleep at night.
4. No, drugs from the streets aren't ever helpful.
5. No, the streets are never a comfortable place to sleep.
6. No, street people aren't usually rich.
7. Yes, they were feeling very alone.

Student Reader

Lesson 15 Continued

Oral Questions   Teacher Guide

ACTIVITY 3: Your teacher will help you make the questions for these answers. Write your questions on the board.

ANSWERS	QUESTIONS
1. This is a street person.	Is…?
2. He is sleeping on a cold bench.	Is…?
3. He is always alone.	Is…?
4. The cold bench is outside.	Is…?
5. There aren't any friendly people nearby.	Are…?
6. He will get very wet when it rains.	Will…?

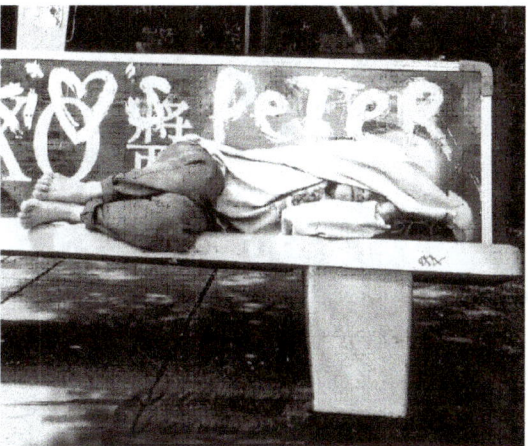

EXERCISES 1 AND 2 – WORKBOOK PAGE 34

ACTIVITY 4: Work in small groups asking and answering the questions. Check your answers. All answers should have a "<u>likely</u>", or a "<u>probably</u>". Notice that "<u>likely</u>" is usually used in the negative answers.

EXAMPLE: How long will you work on your English tonight?
ANSWERS: I'll probably work for about an hour.
I won't likely have time to work on my English tonight.

1. What will you see in town?
2. Will you walk to town?
3. When will you buy a new jacket?
4. When will you have a holiday?
5. How will you get to class tomorrow?
6. Where will you eat supper tonight?
7. Where will you go tomorrow?

1. I'll likely see _____.
2. Yes, I'll probably walk to town.
   No, I won't likely walk to town.
3. I'll probably buy a new jacket next year.
   I won't likely buy a new jacket for a long time.
4. I'll probably have a holiday in _____.
   I won't likely have a holiday this year.
5. I'll probably come (get) to class by helicopter.
   I won't likely come to class by helicopter.
6. I'll probably eat supper at home tonight.
   I won't likely eat any supper tonight.
7. I'll likely go to archery practice.
   I won't likely go to archery practice.

EXERCISE 3 – WORKBOOK PAGE 35
ACTIVITY 5 – Teacher Guide PAGE 43

Student Reader

Lesson 16

VOCABULARY:
living room   brainstorm (to)   newspaper   maybe   else   welcome

ACTIVITY 1:   Listen to the audio your teacher read the passage. . Then take turns reading the sentences orally.

The people on the streets in Victoria know that there is one place where they can go. It is a small building called "The Open Door." The food stores give The Open Door their bread that is one day old.
Many people bring in clothing. Some of this is given to the street people. Volunteer workers help to serve bread, tea and coffee. Each day there are newspapers to read, and a warm place to sit while having coffee and something to eat.. They see their friends, and they talk. They call it their "Living Room".

Student Reader

Lesson 16 Continued

ACTIVITY 2: This is a whole class activity.
Read each question orally and brainstorm as many ideas as possible for each question. Write all the ideas on the board.

1. What are some other ways that people could help the street people?

2. How does working as a volunteer help the person doing the work?

3. Why do you think the street people call The Open Door their "living room"?

ACTIVITY 3: Divide into small groups and decide which idea your group thinks is the best. Then return to the large group and tell the other groups what you decided.

Oral Questions Teacher Guide

EXERCISES 1, 2 AND 3: WORKBOOK PAGE 36

ACTIVITY 4: Ask and answer these questions. Check your answers.

1. What city has a place called "The Open Door"?
2. Who gives The Open Door some day-old bread?
3. What do the people bring to The Open Door?
4. The Open Door is a friendly place ____?
5. Who works at The Open Door?
6. Do volunteer workers get any money?
7. What else can the street people do at The Open Door?
8. Do they see their friends there?
9. What do they call The Open Door?

1. Victoria has The Open Door.
2. The stores give The Open Door some bread.
3. They bring clothes.
4. Isn't it?   Yes, it is.
5. Volunteers work at The Open Door.
6. No, they don't get any money.
7. They can read a newspaper. They can talk to their friends. They can get warm.
8. Yes, they see their friends there.
9. They call it their " Living Room" .

ACTIVITY 5 – WORKBOOK PAGE 37
EXERCISE 4 – WORKBOOK PAGE 37
TEST – GUIDE - PAGES – 46 AND 47

Lesson 17

VOCABULARY:			
prefer (to)	patron	matter (to)	request (to)
tomato	ice cream	pie	wish (to)
chocolate	salad	crowd	dessert
soup	sweet	menu	instead of
beverage	lunchroom	noodles	pineapple
			would

USING "WOULD".

"Would" is a polite way of making a request or asking about someone's wishes.
It is usually used instead of saying: What do you want to have?

EXAMPLE: What would you like?
I would like some coffee, please.

ACTIVITY 1: Listen to your teacher. Then say these contractions orally.

CONTRACTIONS WITH WOULD

I'd = I would you'd = you would he'd = he would she'd = she would
it'd = it would we'd = we would you'd = you would they'd = they would
they wouldn't = they would not

IVY'S LUNCHROOM

Soup and salad	$5.95
Pizza with tomatoes and pineapple	$4.95
Noodles with vegetables	$6.95
Cheese and tomato sandwich	$5.95

BEVERAGES
Hot chocolate	$1.95
Tea or coffee	$1.75
Mango juice	$1.25
Orange juice	$1.25

DESSERTS
Ice cream	$1.75
Pie	$2.50

Student Reader

Lesson 17 Continued

ACTIVITY 2: Listen to your teacher read the dialogue. Note the contractions with "would".

NARRATOR: Carol is in Ivy's Lunchroom with two friends, Zula and Berko from South Africa. They don't speak English. She ordered for them.

WAITER: What would you like today?

CAROL: I'd like to order for my friends.

WAITER: That's fine. What would they like?
CAROL: Zula says she'd like the soup and salad. Berko says he'd like the pizza.

WAITER: And what would you like?
CAROL: I'd like the noodles, please.

WAITER: Would you like something to drink?
CAROL: We'd all like a glass of juice.

WAITER: What kind of juice?
CAROL: They'd like mango juice and I'll have orange juice.

WAITER: It'd take a few minutes to make the orange juice.
CAROL: That wouldn't matter. It'd be okay.

WAITER: Here are your orders.

ACTIVITY 3: Divide into small groups. Role-play the dialogue three or four times, changing roles each time.

ACTIVITY 4: Role-play the Waiter and Carol. Complete the sentences orally.

The waiter isn't sure what they ordered. He checks their order with Carol.
Add a <u>tag question</u> where you see… (Check the sentence tense.) They are in the past tense.

WAITER: Your friend (pointing to Zula) ordered soup and salad, …?

CAROL: Yes, …

WAITER: He (pointing to Berko) ordered a cheese and tomato sandwich, …?

CAROL: No, … He ordered pizza.

WAITER: Thanks. You ordered noodles, …?

CAROL: Yes, …

WAITER: They (pointing to Carol's friends) ordered mango juice, …?

CAROL: Yes, … and I ordered orange juice.

WAITER: Thanks, I'll get it all now.

EXERCISES 1 and 2 – WORKBOOK PAGE 38

Lesson 17 Continued

ACTIVITY 5:
Ask and answer these questions using contractions for the pronoun + would.
Then check your answers.

1. Would you want to order some salad?
2. What would you prefer, pizza or soup?
3. Would you order orange juice?
4. What beverage do you prefer?
5. Would it matter if you had to wait?
6. Would you order ice cream or pie?
7. Do you often order soup?
8. Do you usually order noodles?
9. What kind of pizza would you like?

1. Yes, I'd want to order some salad. / No, I wouldn't want to order any salad.
2. I'd prefer pizza. / I'd prefer soup.
3. Yes, I'd order orange juice. / No, I wouldn't order orange juice.
4. I'd prefer / mango juice / orange juice, tea / coffee / hot chocolate.
5. Yes, it'd matter. / No, it wouldn't matter.
6. I'd order ice cream. / I'd order pie.
7. Yes, I often order soup. / No, I don't often order soup.
8. Yes, I usually order noodles. / No, I don't usually order noodles.
9. I'd like pizza.

Oral Questions Teacher Guide

ACTIVITY 6: Divide into groups of three or four.
One person will be the waiter.
The others (patrons) are ordering some lunch in Ivy's Lunchroom.
Look at the menu and decide what you will have.

Suggested Questions for the waiter:
What would you like to have today?
Would you like some coffee?
Would you like some dessert?

Suggested answers for the patrons:
I'd like some orange juice, please.
I won't have any coffee, thanks.
I'll have the Pizza, please.

NOTE: Sometimes the future "I'll have" is used instead of "I'd like".

EXERCISES 3 AND 4 – WORKBOOK PAGE 39
ACTIVITY 7 - Teacher Guide PAGES 49 AND 50

Lesson 18

VOCABULARY:

such as (for example)	wait (to)	arena	excitement
veggies (vegetables)	animal	other	succeed (to) ice rink
compete in (to)	although	professional	be able (to) language
			climb (to) single

The verbs and adjectives below are often followed by a preposition.
They have a specific meaning.

Phrases using words followed by prepositions:

to wait for a friend	to arrive at class	to ask for help
to talk about a movie	to be interested in sports	across from your house
to sleep in late	to stay up late	to pick up a friend
time-off from work	kind of hamburgers	to compete in sports
dream about playing	such as a national team	to take turns with someone

https://tinyurl.com/bde2ew4n

ACTIVITY 1:
Listen to the audio your teacher read the passage. Then take turns reading the sentences.

Favorite Sports in Canada

Many students in Canada love to compete in different sports. Because Canadian winters are very cold, ice hockey is a favorite. Many schools have small outdoor ice rinks and most towns and cities have indoor arenas and outdoor rinks, too. The students love to compete against other schools and teams from other towns.

Although ice hockey is the favorite sport for boys and many girls, they also like to compete in soccer and basketball games. Sometimes a student who is very good at a sport is able to join a professional team such as the National Hockey League and compete with other countries. Many young students dream about becoming a professional player, but only a few succeed.

ACTIVITY 2:
Divide into groups of two or three. Role-play the dialogue several times, changing roles.

NARRATOR: Brian and Raymond are talking about sports.

BRIAN: I like soccer and hockey but I dream about being a professional soccer player.

RAYMOND: We play soccer in my country but we don't play hockey.

BRIAN: Would you want to be a professional player?

RAYMOND: No, I don't want to compete in games, I prefer hiking and mountain climbing.

BRIAN: I love the excitement!

RAYMOND: The mountains are exciting, too. I never know what animal I'll meet!

ACTIVITY 3 – WORKBOOK PAGE 40

Student Reader

Lesson 18 Continued

Oral Questions Teacher Guide

ACTIVITY 4: Divide into small groups. Ask and answer the questions, then check the answer.

1. Do you often <u>wait for</u> your friend? (no)
2. Did your friend <u>talk about</u> the latest movie? (yes)
3. Are you <u>interested in</u> sports? (yes)
4. Did you <u>stay up</u> late last night? (no)
5. Did you <u>ask for</u> a cup of coffee? (no)
6. Do you <u>arrive at</u> work on time? (yes)
7. Are your friends <u>interested in</u> languages? (yes)
8. Do you often <u>pick up</u> your friend? (yes)
9. Did you get <u>time-off</u> from work yesterday? (no)

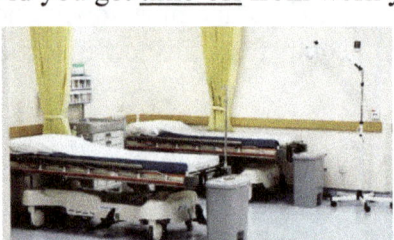

10. Did you <u>sleep in</u> this morning? (no)
11. Do you live <u>across from</u> the hospital? (no)
12. Do you like to <u>compete in</u> games? (yes)

1. No, I don't often wait for my friend.
2. Yes, my friend talked about the latest movie.
3. Yes, I'm interested in sports.
4. No, I didn't stay up late last night.
5. No, I didn't ask for a cup of coffee.
6. Yes, I arrive at work on time.
7. Yes, my friends are interested in languages.
8. Yes, I often pick up my friend.
9. No, I didn't get time-off from work yesterday.
10. No, I didn't sleep in this morning.
11. No, I don't live across from the hospital.
12. Yes, I like to compete in games.

EXERCISES 1 AND 2 – WORKBOOK PAGE 41
REVIEW ACTIVITY 5 – GUIDE PAGES 52 - 54

Student Reader

Lesson 19

VOCABULARY:	form		
chance	break (to)	pocket	so
cookie	got	aloud	rope
must	express (to)	necessary	bow

THE BRITISH USE OF HAVE GOT

NORTH AMERICAN　　　　　　　　　　　　　　　　**BRITISH**
I have a car.　　　　　　　　　　　　　　　　　　　I have got a car.
I've a car.　　　　　　　　　　　　　　　　　　　　I've got a car.

The British "have got" means "have."
The expression "have got" is common in informal spoken British English.
Its meaning is present. It has no past form.
The British use "have got" instead of do - **EXAMPLE:** I don't have a dog. I haven't got a dog.

Using "have got / has got" instead of "have / has".

ACTIVITY 1: Listen to your teacher read each sentence. Then repeat it using "have got"

EXAMPLES:　　She <u>has</u> blond hair.　　　　　　　　She <u>has got</u> blond hair
　　　　　　　　They <u>have</u> a crowded apartment.　　They <u>have got</u> a crowded apartment.

1. He has some a newspaper.
2. They have a chance to travel.
3. The man has a newspaper.
4. The restaurant has many patrons.
5. The students have some juice.
6. The buildings have many windows.
7. The boy has some pie.
8. The mountains have a lot of snow.

EXERCISES 1 - WORKBOOK PAGE 42

CONTRACTIONS WITH "HAVE"				
I have - I've	you have - you've	he has - he's	she has - she's	it has - it's
we have - we've	you have - you've	they have - they've		

Student Reader

Lesson 19 Continued

Oral Questions Teacher Guide

ACTIVITY 2:   **ASK YOUR PARTNER**

Use sentences using "have / has got" with contractions and the negative. Then check your answers.

EXAMPLE: Do you have a cookie?   No, I haven't got a cookie.

1. Do we have many students?
2. Do they have their notebooks?
3. Do you have the chance to travel?
4. Do you have some juice?

5. Do we have time to do this activity?
6. Does she have a yellow sweater?
7. Does she have glasses?
8. Do you have a sister?
9. Do you have a brother?

---

1. Yes, we've got many students.
   No, we haven't got many students.
2. Yes, they've got their notebooks.
   No, they haven't got their notebooks.
3. Yes, I've got the chance to travel.
   No, I haven't got the chance to travel.
4. Yes, I've got some juice.
   No, I haven't got any juice.
5. Yes, we've got time to do this activity.
   No, we haven't got time to do this activity.
6. Yes, she's got a yellow sweater.
   No, she hasn't got a yellow sweater.
7. Yes, she's got glasses.
   No, he hasn't got glasses.
8. Yes, I've got a sister.
   No, I haven't got a sister.
9. Yes, I've got a brother.
   No, I haven't got a brother.

EXERCISE 2 - WORKBOOK PAGE 42
EXERCISE 3 - WORKBOOK PAGE 43

Student Reader

Lesson 19 Continued

EXPRESSING NECESSITY

PRESENT: I have to talk. I must talk - indicates urgency – importance
(<u>must</u> is usually stronger than <u>have to</u>)

PAST: I had to talk. **THERE IS NO PAST FORM FOR: "must"**
THERE IS NO PAST FORM FOR: "have got to"

ACTIVITY 3: Divide into groups of two or three.
Take turns reading aloud and completing the following sentences using:

<u>have / has to</u>,   <u>had to</u>,   <u>must</u>   or   have <u>/ has got to</u> (British form)

Read and answer the sentence, then check your answer.

EXAMPLE: He <u>has to</u> run home.   He <u>must</u> run home.   He <u>has got to</u> run home.

NOTE: The meaning is the same for all three examples.

1. It's late at night so I ….. walk home in the dark.
2. I ….. catch the 10:30 bus. (British form)
3. I ….. pay at the restaurant <u>last night</u>. (past tense)
4. I …. wear small clothes. (British form)
5. When he broke his leg the doctor said he …… go to the hospital. (past tense)
6. When they go hiking they … get home before dark.
7. The patrons in a restaurant … have some money. (British form)
8. She saw a big animal in the forest so she … run fast. (past tense)
9. The street people … find a place to sleep.
10. She … take a taxi to work because she slept in. (past tense)
11. He … get to his soccer game on time. (British form)
12. They …study their English!

1. must / have to / have got to
2. have got to
3. had to
4. have got to
5. had to
6. must / have to
7. have got to
8. had to
9. have to / must
10. had to
11. has got to
12. must / have to

EXERCISE 4 - WORKBOOK PAGE 43
ACTIVITY 4 – Teacher Guide PAGES 57 AND 58

Student Reader

Lesson 20 REVIEW

ACTIVITY 1:   Divide into groups of four.
Role-play the dialogue changing roles two or three times.

NARRATOR: Sarah and Peter are ordering their supper in a restaurant.
WAITER: Hello, would you like to have a menu?
PETER: Yes, please.
NARRATOR: The waiter returns with the menus.

WAITER: The chicken pasta is very good tonight.
SARAH: Thanks, we'll look at the menu fr a few minutes.

PETER: I think I'd like the pizza.
SARAH: I thought you would. You usually order pizza.
PETER: Are you going to order the pasta as usual?
SARAH: No, tonight I'm going to have soup and a salad.

NARRATOR: The waiter returns.
WAITER: Have you decided what you'd like to order?
PETER: Yes, I'd like the ham and pineapple pizza, please.
SARAH: I'd like to have soup and salad.
WAITER: Would you like to have something to drink?
PETER: Yes, we'd like two cups of coffee, please.
NARRATOR: The waiter leaves to get their orders.

ACTIVITY 2: Stay with your group and ask each other these questions several times:
Then check your answers. Remember, you don't use "ever" in a positive sentence.

1. Where are Sarah and Peter?

2. Would you ask the waiter for a menu?

3. Would you ever order chicken pasta?

4. Do you usually look at the menu for a few minutes?

5. Would you want to have soup and salad for supper?

6. What drink would you order?

7. Have you ever worked in a restaurant?

8. Would you ever order pizza?

---

1. They are in a restaurant.

2. Yes, I'd ask the waiter for a menu.
   No, I wouldn't ask the waiter for a menu.

3. Yes, I'd order chicken pasta.
   No, I wouldn't ever order chicken pasta.

4. Yes, I usually look at the menu for a few minutes.
   No, I don't usually look at the menu for a few minutes.

5. Yes, I'd want to have soup and salad for supper.
   No, I wouldn't want to have soup and salad for supper.

6. I'd order _____.

7. Yes, I've worked in a restaurant.
   No, I haven't ever worked in a restaurant.

8. Yes, I'd order pizza.
   No, I wouldn't ever order pizza.

EXERCISE 1 – WORKBOOK PAGE 44

Student Reader

Lesson 20 Continued

ACTIVITY 3: Divide into groups of two or three. Ask each other these questions. Check your answers.

1. What do you like the best, tennis, reading or swimming?
2. What sports are you the most interested in?
3. Do you play a lot of soccer?
4. What country has the most people, United States, Argentina or China?
5. Is India hotter than Antarctica?
6. Do you like hot countries better than cold countries?
7. What is the worst way to travel?
8. Which country has the fewest people, Antarctica or the United States?
9. Are you the tallest in your family?
10. Are you older than your friend?
11. Did you get up earlier than usual this morning?
12. Are you the youngest in your family?

---

1. I like _____ the best.
2. I'm the most interested in _____.
3. Yes, I play a lot of soccer.
   No, I don't play soccer.
4. China has the most people.
5. Yes, India is hotter than Antarctica.
6. Yes, I like hot countries better than cold countries.
   No, I don't like hot countries better than cold countries.
7. Traveling by _____ is the worst (way to travel).
8. Antarctica has the fewest people.
9. Yes, I'm the tallest in my family.
   No, I'm not the tallest in my family.
10. Yes, I'm older than my friend.
    No, I'm not older than my friend.
11. Yes, I got up earlier than usual this morning.
    No, I didn't get up earlier than usual this morning
12. Yes, I'm the youngest in my family.
    No, I'm not the youngest in my family.

Oral Questions Teacher Guide

MID-TERM - TEST 5 PAGES 61 - 64
EXERCISES 2, 3 AND 4 – WORKBOOK PAGE 45
Note: A film is a movie.

THE GOATS

Two goats found a film behind a theater. The first goat ate the film.

Second goat: How was the film?

First goat: The film was okay, but I liked the book better.

Student Reader

High Beginners ESL Lesson Plans Book 1

A Conversational Approach

Student Workbook

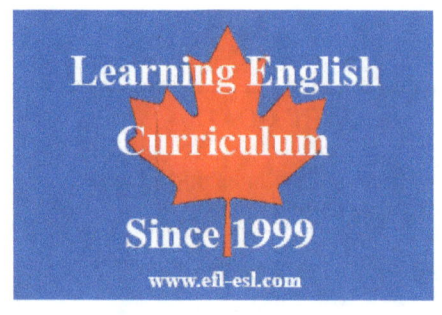

Daisy A. Stocker B.Ed., M.Ed.
George A Stocker D.D.S.

Lesson 1

EXERCISE 1

One day Silvia and Ronald talk about going to a movie.
Write their words in the correct order.
Remember the punctuation - . ? !
Sentences begin with a capital letter.

Ronald: There a town good Silvia is movie in .

Silvia: know I . _____

Ronald: Can tonight we go ? _____

Silvia: Saturday can I on night go . _____

Ronald: great is That ! _____

Silvia: can What go time we ? _____

Ronald: eight How o'clock about ? _____

Silvia: great That's Ronald. Thanks ! _____

EXERCISE 2:   MATCH THE MEANING

time-off _____

to note _____

to love _____

to think _____

a movie _____

legs _____

to have an idea about something   you don't have to work   you watch it
to like something / someone very much   you want to remember it   you walk with them

NOTE: Ronald says "eight o'clock". We know he is talking about the evening because we don't usually go to the movies at eight in the morning.

Student Workbook

Lesson 1 Continued

BINGO

ACTIVITY 4: **MATCH THE MEANING**
Some of the verbs match the infinitive of the verb to the past tense.

LIST 1: **PRINT THESE WORDS**

to start	morning	to travel	a nurse
legs	an actress	to tell	to leave
to know	to stay	will not	to visit
nearby	noon	to return	to give
clothes	to sleep	to laugh	to listen
notebook	time-off	to say	road

LIST 2: **WORDS TO CALL**

1 works in a hospital	7 told	13 left	19 knew
2 12:00 o'clock	8 returned	14 gave	20 slept
3 you walk along it	9 A.M.	15 traveled	21 stayed
4 you walk with them	10 won't	16 visited	22 near to you
5 works in a theater	11 you wear them	17 laughed	23 listened
6 you write in it	12 you don't go to work	18 said	24 started

Student Workbook

Lesson 2

EXERCISE 1: ANSWER IN SENTENCES. USE PRONOUNS IN YOUR ANSWERS.
EXAMPLE: How many children do <u>Jim and Janet</u> have? <u>They</u> have two children.

1. Who are Jim, Janet, Pam and Brian going to pick up?
   _____

2. How will Jim and his family get to the airport?
   _____

3. Who is Craig's brother?
   _____

4. Who are Ruth and Raymond's cousins?
   _____

5. Where are Ruth and Raymond from?
   _____

6. Where are Ruth and Raymond going?
   _____

7. How will they travel from Melbourne to Sydney?
   _____

8. How will they travel from Sydney to Vancouver?
   _____

9. Where do Jim, Janet, Pam and Brian live?
   _____

10. Who is younger than Raymond?
    _____

11. Who is older than Ruth?
    _____

Student Workbook

Lesson 2 Continued

ACTIVITY 4: ASK A PARTNER THESE QUESTIONS. USE REPORTED SPEECH.
Write his or her answers

EXAMPLE: What did you have for supper? _____ had chicken for supper.

1. What did you have for breakfast? _____

2. Did you come to class by motorcycle? _____

3. Do you go swimming in December? _____

4. Do you wear a coat in January? _____

5. Do you have a holiday in July? _____

6. Did you get time-off from work today? _____

7. Do you have a birthday in June? _____

8. Were you born on December 31st? _____

ACTIVITY 5: ASK OTHER STUDENTS

EXAMPLE: <u>Robert</u> was born in <u>May</u>.   He was born on <u>the twenty-fifth of May</u>.
What month were you born?   What day were you born?

FIRST FRIEND

_____ was born in _____.

FIRST FRIEND

She/he was born on _____.

SECOND FRIEND

_____ was born in _____.

SECOND FRIEND

She/he was born on _____.

THIRD FRIEND

_____ was born in _____.

THIRD FRIEND

She/he was born on _____.

FOURTH FRIEND

_____ was born in _____.

FOURTH FRIEND

She/he was born on _____.

Student Workbook

Lesson 3

EXERCISE 1:   Write the tag question.   Answer the tag question.

1. You <u>were</u> in English class, _____? _____

2. You <u>can't</u> ride a bicycle, _____? _____

3. You <u>have</u> a home, _____? _____

4. She <u>wasn't</u> a student, _____? _____

5. They <u>aren't</u> in town? _____? _____

6. It <u>is</u> cold today, _____? _____

7. They <u>can</u> get a bus, _____? _____

8. Flowers <u>can</u> grow, _____? _____

9. India <u>is</u> a big country, _____? _____

The verb "to do" is used to form the tag question with most other verbs.
Exceptions: be, have, can (as above)
(will, future tense)
could, would, should, must, (to be introduced later)

USING <u>DO</u> IN A TAG QUESTION

EXAMPLES: They **don't** live here, **do** they?   No, they **don't**.

He **doesn't** play football, **does** he?   No, he **doesn't**.
She **likes** to swim, **doesn't** she?   Yes, she **does**.
You **played** basketball yesterday, **didn't** you?   Yes, I **did**.

EXERCISE 2:   Tag questions   Answers
Remember to match the tense.   They <u>worked</u> here, <u>didn't</u> they?   Yes, they <u>did</u>.

1. George lives here, _____? _____

2. Dogs don't read, _____? _____

3. They came here, _____? _____

4. You listen to music, _____? _____

5. You don't sleep at noon, _____? _____

6. We visited their friends, _____? _____

Student Workbook

Lesson 3 Continued

ACTIVITY 4:   **TAG QUESTIONS**
Ask your partner the question and add the tag.
Your partner will <u>say</u> the answer.
You and your partner write the tag and the answer.

Tag questions	Answers
1. This isn't your birthday, _____?	_____
2. You have a book, _____?	_____
3. You're a student, _____?	_____
4. You have a pen, _____?	_____
5. You weren't born in 2000, _____?	_____
6. You can get a bus, _____?	_____
7. You like music, _____?	_____

EXERCISE 3:   Put these words in the correct order.
Remember to put <u>when something happens</u> at the end of the sentence.

EXAMPLE: He goes to bed <u>at night</u>.

1. working, She, mornings, in, is, the.
   _____

2. house, in, They, evenings, meet, the, at, his.
   _____

3. night, watched, home, They, last, at, television.
   _____

4. notebook, She, in, yesterday, her, wrote.
   _____

5. them, school, dog, The, followed, to, morning, this.
   _____

6. has, dress, a, Marietta, beautiful, hasn't, she?
   _____

7. has, she, Yes _____

Student Workbook

Lesson 4

EXERCISE 1:   Complete using – this, these, that, those

1. _____ small car is far away.
2. _____ three birds are near.
3. _____ big car is nearer.
4. _____ two birds are farther away.

EXERCISE 2:   Complete the question and write the answer.

1. The big car is near us, _____?   Yes, _____.
2. The three birds are near the big car, _____?   Yes, _____.
3. There are three birds near us, _____ there?   _____ there _____.
4. The small car isn't near us, _____?   No, _____.
5. There is one small car, _____?   _____.

EXERCISE 3:

TAG QUESTIONS:

1. The boats are in the water, _____?

   ANSWER: _____

2. The boats aren't near the elephants, _____?

   ANSWER: _____

3. The old man is beside the bicycle, _____?

   ANSWER: _____

4. The girl is on the bicycle, _____?

   ANSWER: _____

5. The girl can ride the bicycle, _____?

   ANSWER: _____

6. The man is close to the lady, _____?

   ANSWER: _____

7. The man is beside the lady, _____?

   ANSWER: _____

8. They are dressed formally, _____?

   ANSWER: _____

Student Workbook

Lesson 4 Continued

9. The elephants aren't in the water, _____?

   ANSWER: _____

10. The elephants can't ride a bicycle, _____?

    ANSWER: _____

11. They aren't black, _____?

    ANSWER: _____

EXERCISE 4:   **Answer in sentences.**

1. Do you live far from here?
   _____

2. Did you get time-off from work last week?
   _____

3. Do you love to buy new clothes?
   _____

4. Which movie did you like the best?
   _____

5. Are you going to listen to music today?
   _____

ACTIVITY 1:   Give each student one role card from page 12 of the Guide.
The students are to ask two other students the questions on the information sheet.

INFORMATION SHEET: (Answer in sentences using: <u>in</u> or <u>on</u>.)

What is your full name? _____

What month were you born in? _____

What day were you born on? _____

****

What is your full name? _____

What month were you born in? _____

What day were you born on? _____

Student Workbook

LESSON 5

ACTIVITY 3: Talk to three students, ask them where they live and write their answers.

EXAMPLE:
- **You ask:** "Fred, do you live near the English School?"
- **Student:** "No, I live far from the English School." *or* "Yes, I live near the English School."
- **You ask:** "How far from the English School do you live, Fred?"
- **Student:** " I live 3 kilometers from the English School."

QUESTIONNAIRE: (name) Fred lives 3 kilometers from the English School.
EXAMPLE: He lives <u>farther from</u> the English School <u>than</u> I do.
or He lives <u>nearer to</u> the English School <u>than</u> I do.

Now complete the questionnaire.

1. (name)_____ lives _____ the English School.

   He / she lives _____ I do.

2. (name)_____ lives _____ the English School.

   He / she lives _____ I do.

3. (name)_____ lives _____ the English School.

   He / she lives _____ I do.

EXERCISE 1: Put these words in the correct order to make a sentence.

1. one, Melanie, the, English School, lives, from, kilometer

   _____

2. the, English School, Jim, from, lives, ten, kilometers

   _____

3. to, John, Melanie, the, English School, nearer, lives, than

   _____

4. John, as, as, lives, the, English School, far, from Pamela

   _____

5. the, English School, lives, the, Jim, farthest, from

   _____

Student Workbook

Lesson 5 Continued

EXERCISE 2:

Melanie lives 1 kilometer from the English School.
John lives 3 kilometers from the English School.
Pamela lives 3 kilometers from the English School.
Jim lives 10 kilometers from the English School.

Melanie lives <u>nearer to</u> the English School <u>than</u> John.
Melanie lives <u>closer to</u> the English School <u>than</u> John.

NOTE The meaning is the same.

Pamela and John live <u>the same distance from</u> the English School.
Pamela lives <u>the same distance from</u> the English School <u>as</u> John.
Pamela lives <u>as far from</u> the English School <u>as</u> John.

NOTE The meaning is the same.

Jim lives <u>the farthest from</u> the English School.

Answer these questions in sentences:

1. Who lives closer to the English School than Pamela?

2. Who lives farther from the English School than John?

3. Who lives the same distance from the English School as John?

4. Who lives the closest to the English School?

5. Who lives the same distance from the English School as you?

6. Do you live farther from the English School than Jim?

7. Do you live closer to the English School than Melanie?

8. Do you live the same distance from the English School as Pamela?

9. Do you live as near to (as close to) the English School as Melanie?

10. Do you live farther from the English School than Pamela?

Student Workbook

Lesson 5 Continued

BINGO

ACTIVITY 4:
Match the meaning: Before playing Bingo, the students are to put the number of the words in LIST 1, beside the correct meaning in LIST 2.

EXAMPLE: 10 - the day after Tuesday

LIST 1:   **WORDS TO WRITE IN THE SQUARES:**

1 beside	6 close	11 breakfast	16 holiday	21 basketball
2 to return	7 two thirty	12 clothes	17 teacher	22 music
3 bicycle	8 hospital	13 old	18 weekend	23 elephant
4 greater than	9 Thursday	14 airport	19 tomorrow	24 today
5 December	10 Wednesday	15 younger	20 ten thirty	

LIST 2:   **WORDS TO CALL:**

10 the day after Tuesday	you don't work	food in the morning	this day
works in a school	the last month	where a plane goes	not as old as
half past ten	you listen to it	not far	you wear them
to come back	bigger than	Saturday and Sunday	not young
next to	played with a ball	doctors work there	half past two
the next day	a big animal	day after Wednesday	you ride it

Student Workbook

Lesson 6

EXERCISE 1: Complete the dialogue. You decide what Raymond and Ruth say. Talk about Australia's summer in January and winter in July.

Narrator: Raymond, Ruth, Brian and Pam are talking about the new department store that has opened in Brian and Pam's Canadian city.

Raymond: I hear you have a new department store here. What _____?

Brian: They have many things. I went to their sports department yesterday.

Pam: I was there, too.

Ruth: I'm interested in _____.

Pam: Our stores have clothes for cold weather, hot rainy weather and beautiful warm weather.

Brian: They have mountain bicycles, too.

Ruth: You have hot summers, _____?

Pam: Yes, some places in Canada have very hot summers.

Raymond: Our winters _____.

Pam: Our cold winters give us great sports.

Brian: I love winter sports!

ACTIVITY 5:   **FIND A PARTNER**

ASK EACH OTHER THESE QUESTIONS   USE REPORTED SPEECH.
EXAMPLE: John, do you play soccer?   John plays soccer.   John doesn't play soccer.

1. Do you like soccer <u>more than</u> basketball?

   _____

2. Do you like hiking <u>more than</u> swimming?

   _____

3. What do you think is <u>the best</u>, sports, reading or music?

   _____

4. What are you <u>the most</u> interested in?

   _____

5. Do you think that cold weather is <u>better than</u> hot weather?

   _____

6. What do you do <u>the most</u> often, read, hike or watch TV?

   _____

Student Workbook

Lesson 6 Continued

EXERCISE 2:   Answer these questions in sentences.

1. What city are Ruth and Raymond from?
   _____

2. Does India have <u>more</u> people <u>than</u> Canada? (yes)
   _____

3. Which country has <u>the most</u> people, Australia, India or Canada? (India)
   _____

4. Are many people in your country <u>interested in</u> soccer?
   _____

5. Are women <u>more</u> interested in clothes <u>than</u> men?
   _____

6. Are international games <u>more</u> exciting <u>than</u> home team games?
   _____

7. What sports are you <u>interested in</u>?
   _____

EXERCISE 3:   **MATCH THE MEANING**

department store   _____

international   _____

birthday   _____

sports   _____

winter   _____

summer   _____

weather   _____

close to   _____

etcetera = etc.   _____

sun   _____

activities like soccer, swimming, archery etc.   the hot time of year
a store that sells many things – food, clothes etc. the cold time of year
it means more of the same kind of things   near to
all the countries of the world   the day you were born
it keeps us warm   rain, snow, sun etc.

Student Workbook   13

EXERCISE 1:

Lesson 7

Answer in sentences.

Ruth and Pam went to a big store where the clothes were cheap but not good. Next they went to a smaller better store, and the clothes were more expensive. Then they went to the smallest store where the beautiful clothes were the most expensive.

1. Which store had the cheapest clothes?

   _____

2. Which store had the most expensive clothes?

   _____

3. Were the cheap clothes the best?

   _____

4. Did the smallest store have the cheapest clothes?

   _____

5. Were the beautiful clothes more expensive than the cheap clothes?

   _____

6. Do you think that the cheapest clothes are the best?

   _____

Raymond has a bicycle, Brian has a motorcycle, and Brian's father has a sports car.

7. Who can go the fastest?

   _____

8. Can Brian go faster than his father can?

   _____

9. Can Raymond go faster than Brian can?

   _____

10. Who goes the slowest?

    _____

11. Does Raymond go slower than Brian's father does?

    _____

12. Can a bicycle go as fast as a car?

    _____

13. What do you want to have?

    _____

Lesson 7 Continued

EXERCISE 2: Complete the sentences using these words.
fast, for, interested, faster than, about, the fastest

The boys didn't go shopping _____ clothes.

They talked _____ things that boys are _____ in.

Raymond has a bicycle. He can't go very _____.

Brian has a motorcycle. It can go _____ _____ Raymond's bicycle.

Brian's father has a Mercedes sports car. He can go _____ _____.

ACTIVITY 5:
Ask a partner these questions and write their answers using reported speech.
The words in the (brackets) will help you with your answers.

1. Do you live closer to the school than I do? *(closer to, farther from)*

   _____ lives _____ _____ the school than I do.
2. Did you get to class earlier than I did? *(earlier than, later than)*

   _____ got to class_____ _____ I did.
3. Are you taller than I am? *(taller than, not as tall as)*

   _____ I am.
4. Are you shorter than I am *(shorter than, not as short as, taller than)*

   _____ I am.

EXERCISE 3: Answer in sentences.

1. Is today hotter than yesterday? *(hotter than)*

   Yes, today is _____ _____ yesterday.

   OR No, today isn't _____ _____ yesterday.
2. Is a car bigger than a train? *(bigger than or smaller than)*

   A _____ is _____ _____ _____ a _____.
3. What goes the fastest, a bicycle, a car, or an airplane? *(the fastest)*

   An _____ goes _____ _____.
4. What is the most expensive, a pencil, a bicycle, or a car? *(the most expensive)*

   _____ _____ is _____ _____ _____.
5. What is the least expensive, a pencil, a bicycle, or a car? *(the least expensive)*

   A _____ is _____ _____ _____.

Student Workbook

Lesson 8 REVIEW

EXERCISE 1:

Use any of these comparatives when describing the following.
Add "ing" to the underlined word to start your sentence. (Gerunds will be introduced later.)

the best   the least   the worst   better than   the fastest   the slowest   not as good as

EXAMPLE: You arrive after the movie begins.
Arriving after the movie begins is <u>the worst</u>.

1. You <u>travel</u> by plane.
   _____

2. You <u>travel</u> by train.
   _____

3. You <u>travel</u> by bicycle.
   _____

4. You <u>eat</u> a hot dog.
   _____

5. You <u>drink</u> a lot of cold juice.
   _____

6. You <u>drive</u> a motorcycle.
   _____

7. You <u>ski</u> to class.
   _____

EXERCISE 2:   Make comparative sentences for the following.
EXAMPLES: A boy is <u>lighter than</u> a man is.   This is <u>the longest</u> lesson.

1. Did you come to class _____ _____ your friend did?   (early)

2. Are you _____ _____ you were this morning?   (hungry)

3. Are you _____ _____ your friend?   (tall)

4. Are you _____ _____ in your family?   (young)

5. Walking is _____ _____ way to travel.   (slow)

7. Russia is _____ _____ country.   (big)

8. A train is _____ _____ a bicycle.   (heavy)

9. Skiing is _____ _____ walking.   (fast)

Student Workbook

Lesson 8 Continued

ACTIVITY 2:
ASK YOUR PARTNER   Answer using your partner's name

EXAMPLE: **Do you live closer to the school than I do?**
Yes, _____ lives closer to the school than I do.
No, _____ doesn't live closer to the school than I do.

1. How far from the school do you live?

2. Do you live farther from the school than I do?

3. Do you live nearer to the school than I do?

4. Who lives the farthest from the school?

5. Who lives the nearest to the school?

6. Is the school close to your home?

7. Which is closer to your home, a theater or a church?

8. Are you as tall as your father?

9. Are you taller than I am?

10. Are you the shortest in your family?

11. Do you have more books than I do?

12. Who has the most books?

13. Is your town as big as New York?

Student Workbook

Lesson 8 Continued

ACTIVITY 3:

BINGO
MATCH THE MEANING:
Before playing Bingo, the students are to put the number of the words in LIST 1 beside the correct meaning in LIST 2.

LIST 1 — WORDS TO PRINT

1 weekend	7 far	13 time-off	19 early
2 hot	8 many	14 slow	20 narrow
3 birthday	9 cousin	15 the least	21 month
4 clothes	10 big	16 expensive	22 Canada
5 neighbors	11 noon	17 evening	23 late
6 a few	12 week	18 tomorrow	24 tall

LIST 2 — WORDS TO CALL

___ opposite of cold	___ the next day	___ opposite of short
___ something is a lot of money.	___ It has seven days	___ a long way off
___ They live near you.	___ 12:00	___ not fast
___ The day you were born.	___ a lot	___ opposite of small
1 Saturday and Sunday	___ days you don't work	___ thirty (one) days
___ a country	___ the fewest	___ you wear them
___ your relative	___ opposite of wide	___ not many
___ opposite of early	___ opposite of late	___ 7:00 to 11:00 PM

		BINGO		

Student Workbook

18

Lesson 9

EXERCISE 1:

1. Where did Pam, Brian, Raymond and Ruth go?

   _____

2. Does Brian think that Toto is a smart dog?

   _____

3. What did they take for lunch?

   _____

4. Who ate the most?

   _____

5. Did they have a good time?

   _____

EXERCISE 2: Write comparative sentences using the following words:
Canada / South Africa / better / forests

EXAMPLE: Canada has better forests than South Africa.

NOTE Some words will need to be changed.   **EXAMPLE:** few – fewer, hot - hotter
Remember to add the verbs and prepositions.

1. beautiful buildings / London / Calcutta / more

   _____

2. mountains / Switzerland / France / higher

   _____

3. faster, Horses, run, dogs

   _____

4. Canada / larger / Italy

   _____

5. Spanish / hockey players / the worst

   _____

6. Antarctica / colder/ South America

   _____

7. Melbourne / fewer / London / people

   _____

8. Southern India / hot / Canada

   _____

Student Workbook

Lesson 9 Continued

EXERCISE 3: Use a comparison when answering the following questions in sentences.
Remember: <u>the</u>, <u>than</u>, <u>as</u> where necessary.

1. Is this a good time of year? This is ...   (worst / best)
   _____

2. What do you think about January? January is ...   (best / worst / coldest)
   _____

3. What do you think about winter in Northern Canada? Winter is... (hotter / colder)
   _____

4. What country don't you like? I don't like ...   (as well as)
   _____

5. What do you think about Russia? Russia is ...   (biggest)
   _____

EXERCISE 4: Use these words to complete the paragraphs.
the best   more   cousins   the most   from   in   interested in

Brian and Pam's _____, Raymond and Ruth, are visiting them in Canada.

They are _____ Melbourne, Australia. They are having a good time visiting the lakes

and the department stores. Ruth is interested _____ new clothes, but Pam is _____

interested in sports. Pam thinks the sports equipment, shoes and sports clothes are

_____ _____ interesting. Ruth wants to look at all the clothes.

Brian is _____ _____ the soccer equipment but Raymond likes the many

kinds of sports clothes _____ _____.

EXERCISE 5: Write sentences that answer the questions.
1. Do people drink tea beside the rivers in your town?
   _____

2. Do you like cheese and pickle sandwiches?
   _____

3. Do you like a restaurant better than a picnic?
   _____

4. Do people in your country eat sandwiches?
   _____

Student Workbook

Lesson 10

EXERCISE 1: **Make sentences from the following words, using the correct word order.**

1. supper, He, for, hamburgers, eats, big

   _____

2. week, dog, I, a, big, black, last, saw

   _____

3. girls, Three, went, beautiful, theater, to, the

   _____

4. black, saw, yesterday, big, in, town, a, I, car

   _____

5. red, He, a, T-shirt, had, cotton

   _____

EXERCISE 2: Answer the following questions using <u>two adjectives</u> in your answer.

EXAMPLE: What bathing suits did you see?   *I saw two blue bathing suits.*

Suggested adjectives: colorful   big,   small,   young,
                             old,   best,   nice,   good,   red,   black,   new

1. What did you wear to town yesterday? (past - wore)

   _____

2. What car did you see today?

   _____

3. What did your friend wear today?

   _____

4. What bird did you see today?

   _____

ACTIVITY 2:   **FIND A PARTNER:**
Brainstorm a list of adjectives that describe your classmates.
Divide into groups of two or three.
Next write three sentences that describe another person in your group.
Read your descriptions to each other.
EXAMPLE: She has long brown hair.
Her glasses make her look smart.
She looks nice.

_____

_____

_____

Student Workbook

Lesson 10 Continued

EXERCISE 3: USE ADJECTIVES WHEN ANSWERING IN SENTENCES.

EXAMPLE: Are there many flowers?   *There are many <u>colorful</u> flowers.*

Suggested adjectives: colorful   big   small   young   smart
nice   good   hot   old   best

1. Are there many birds in the parks here?
   _____

2. Are there many people in Paris?
   _____

3. Are there many students here?
   _____

4. Is there some coffee on the table?
   _____

5. Are there soccer players in your country?
   _____

ACTIVITY 3:
DIRECTIONS: Every student is to put his/ her name on a piece of paper.
When all of the papers are put into a box each student is to take one.
If a student takes his/her own name from the box then he/she is to return it and choose another.
Each student is to write a description of the person whose name they selected.
These can be read to the whole class or read individually to the person described.

_____
_____
_____

SUGGESTED ADJECTIVES:
Many of these words will be new to you.
Work together to find their meanings in your class dictionary.
Then write the new words into your glossary.

handsome	beautiful	intelligent	witty
talkative	musical	athletic	artistic
hard working	kindly	courteous	considerate
	caring	peaceful	quiet

Student Workbook

Lesson 10 Continued

EXERCISE 4: REVIEW
MAKE QUESTIONS USING "GOING TO _____" ?

EXAMPLE: What / see   What am I going to see?

1. What / find   _____

2. Who / see   _____

3. When / know   _____

4. What / need   _____

5. Where / live   _____

6. Who / tell   _____

7. When / return   _____

8. Where / go   _____

ACTIVITY 4:   FIND A PARTNER.
Ask each other these questions.
Answer using reported speech.

EXAMPLE: Do you like cheese sandwiches?   _____ likes cheese sandwiches.

1. Do you have a pen in your hand?

   _____

2. Did you get time-off from work last week?

   _____

3. Do you love to buy new clothes?

   _____

4. Which color do you like the best?

   _____

5. Are you going to go to the park today?

   _____

6. Do you have brown hair?

   _____

Student Workbook   23

Lesson 11

EXERCISE 1: Answer in sentences using an adverb from the vocabulary list.

1. How do you cross the street? _____
2. How do you talk to old people? _____
3. How do you work? _____
4. How does a plane travel? _____
5. How does an old man walk? _____
6. How do you eat supper? _____

EXERCISE 2: Complete the following sentences.

EXAMPLE: The dogs were very <u>hungry</u>.   They ate hungrily.

1. They were <u>busy</u> with their work.   They worked _____.
2. The man was extremely <u>heavy</u> and fat.   He moved _____.
3. The buses left every <u>hour</u>.   The buses left _____.
4. Her words were very <u>sad</u>.   She talked _____.
5. He did <u>nice</u> work.   He worked _____.
6. The girl was <u>glad</u> to take the job.   She took it _____.
7. Each piece of bread was <u>thin</u>.   The bread was cut _____.
8. He washes every <u>night</u>.   He washes _____.

ACTIVITY 1: USING "<u>WELL</u>"

"Well" is an adverb. It describes a verb to tell how something is done.

ASK YOUR PARTNER: Use <u>well</u>, <u>very well</u>, or <u>do not</u> _____ <u>very well</u>

Answer using the pronoun <u>He</u> or <u>She</u>

1. How do you play basketball?

_____

2. How do you sing?

_____

3. How do you ride a bicycle?

_____

4. How do you sleep?

_____

Student Workbook

Lesson 11 Continued

EXERCISE 3:

Choose the appropriate adverb to complete the sentences.

sadly	gladly	badly	very	well
extremely	hungrily	slowly	beautifully	

1. They cut the bread _____ thinly.

2. She had her hair cut _____ short.

3. They hadn't eaten since breakfast so they ate _____.

4. The girl was _____ tired so she walked _____.

5. He didn't have a good day because things were going _____.

6. He was kind to her so she helped him _____.

7. Her friend was _____ sad, so she walked home _____.

8. The children looked beautiful, they ran _____.

ACTIVITY 2: **FIND A PARTNER**

Write two sentences about each picture:
Use an adverb or an adjective in each sentence.

_____

_____

_____

_____

_____

Student Workbook

Lesson 11 Continued

ACTIVITY 3:   **BINGO**

Before playing the game, write the number of the word in LIST 1 beside the word with the opposite meaning in List 2.

MATCH THE OPPOSITES

LIST 1:   **WORDS TO PRINT**

1 fast	6 young	11 smart	16 cold	21 love
2 tall	7 walk	12 good	17 sun	22 small
3 blue eyes	8 the most	13 heavy	18 black	23 morning
4 aunt	9 brother	14 mother	19 night	24 last
5 the best	10 happy	15 outside	20 well dressed	

LIST 2:   **WORDS TO CALL**

rain	inside	sad	the worst	first
stupid	big	white	1 slow	old
hate	the least	run	short	bad
brown eyes	hot	light	evening	uncle
sister	father	day	badly dressed	

		BINGO		

Student Workbook

Lesson 12   REVIEW

EXERCISE 1: Answer the questions using one of the adverbs in the (brackets).

1. How do you think he sings? (joyfully, beautifully, sadly, loudly)

   _____

2. How is he dressed? (formally, informally)

   _____

3. How do you think he sings?
   (loudly, softly)

   _____

4. How do you think she moves?
   (slowly, joyfully, quickly)

   _____

5. How do they dress? (formally, informally)

   _____

6. How do you think they dance?
   (beautifully, heavily, slowly)?

   _____

7. How do you think she dances?
   (happily, joyfully)

   _____

8. How is she dressed?
   (formally, informally)

   _____

9. How does the turtle run? (quickly,

   _____

   _____

10. How does he work? (carefully, sadly, happily)

    _____

Student Workbook

Lesson 12 Continued

EXERCISE 2: Put the words in the right sentence order.

1. have, jacket, Do, a, red, you, ?
_____

2. black, has, long, She, hair
_____

3. small, She, hat, a, has
_____

4. T-shirt, colorful, wore, He, a
_____

5. blue, They, shirts, wanted, cotton
_____

EXERCISE 3: Compare Picture 1 and Picture 2 using comparative words.

PICTURE 1   PICTURE 2

Answer in sentences.

1. Which picture has the fewest people?
_____

2. Which picture has the most students pulling in the tug-of-war?
_____

3. Which picture has the most people watching?
_____

4. In which picture does the strongest guy have a red T-shirt?
_____

Student Workbook

Lesson 13

> 1) Put mid-sentence adverbs <u>in front of</u> simple present and simple past verbs.
> Anne <u>always comes</u> on time.

EXERCISE

NOTE

Put the frequency adverbs into the correct position.
The following sentences <u>don't</u> use the verb <u>to be</u>.

1. Jim takes the bus to work. (always) _____

2. Brent plays soccer on Saturdays. (usually) _____

3. Maria likes to play basketball. (always) _____

4. John cooks dinner. (often) _____

5. Sarah dresses casually. (generally) _____

6. Raymond rides on horses. (never) _____

7. Penny phones her friend. (frequently) _____

8. Lucy had a party. (just) _____

9. Ben goes swimming. (hardly ever) _____

10. Mark went walking. (just) _____

11. Lewis wore a T-shirt. (probably) _____

12. Maria buys a train ticket. (sometimes) _____

13. Alexander travels to Canada. (often) _____

14. Bob goes to the movies on Saturdays. (always) _____

15. Is Maria wearing a mask? _____

Student Workbook

Lesson 13 Continued

EXERCISE 2:   USING ADVERBS

Write sentence answers to the following questions. Use a mid-sentence adverb from Page 22

EXAMPLE: Do you wear green?   I <u>hardly ever</u> wear green.

1. Do you eat pizza?   _____
2. Do you play basketball?   _____
3. Do you stay up all night?   _____
4. Do you go swimming?   _____
5. Do you get hungry at noon?   _____
6. Do you meet your friends at the lake?   _____
7. Do you eat Chinese food?   _____
8. Do you eat breakfast in a restaurant?   _____
9. Do you buy expensive clothes?   _____
10. Do you pick up your friends in a car?   _____
11. Do you sleep at home?   _____
12. Do you enjoy eating vegetables?   _____

EXERCISE 3:   MATCH THE MEANING

to dress   _____

to stay up   _____

frequently   _____

hardly ever   _____

occasionally   _____

probably   _____

vegetables   _____

to go out   _____

different   _____

| not the same | you eat them | often | sometimes | to leave |
| to put clothes on | to go to bed late | seldom | likely | |

Student Workbook

Lesson 13 Continued

ACTIVITY 4:   **BINGO**

Before starting to play, write the numbers from LIST 2 beside the word with the same meaning in LIST 1.

EXAMPLE: 1. to go away - 1. to leave

LIST 1:   **PRINT THESE WORDS:**

frequently	seldom	likely	generally
sometimes	finally	badly	slowly
hourly	monthly	thinly	quickly
sadly	nightly	extremely polite	a piece
to agree	the least	to sing well	close to
expensive	to start	time-off	1. to leave

LIST 2:   **CALL THESE WORDS:**

1. to go away	7. free time	13. to begin	19. it costs a lot
2. often	8. hardly ever	14. probably	20. occasionally
3. at last	9. not well	15. not fast	21. once an hour
4. once a month	10. not thick	16. fast	22. not happily
5. every night	11. very polite	17. a good singer	23. a little of something
6. to say "yes"	12. the fewest	18. near	24. usually

		BINGO		

Student Workbook

Lesson 14

EXERCISE 1: Write the questions and answers. Use "ever" or "didn't ever" where necessary. Look at the first word in each question and use the same tense. "never" can be used.

1.

   Did _____?

   _____

2.

   Do _____?

   _____

3.

   Did _____?

   _____

4.

   Do _____?

   _____

5.

   Did _____forest?

   _____

6.

   Did _____?

   _____

7.

   Did _____?

   _____

8. Did _____dragon?

   _____

Student Workbook   32

Lesson 14 Continued

EXERCISE 2: WHAT IS YOUR FAVORITE DAY OF THE YEAR?
Write the answers to these questions using one of the underlined adverbs.

EXAMPLE: My favorite day is my birthday / name day /...
I <u>generally</u> go to the movies on my favorite day. (present tense)

1. What do you <u>usually</u> / <u>often</u> / <u>sometimes</u> do on your favorite day?
   _____

2. What do you <u>generally</u> / <u>frequently</u> / <u>occasionally</u> eat ?
   _____

3. What do you <u>often</u> / <u>usually</u> drink ?
   _____

4. Where do you <u>occasionally</u> / <u>frequently</u> go?
   _____

5. Who do you <u>usually</u> / <u>generally</u> talk to?
   _____

6. Do you <u>generally</u> / <u>sometimes</u> go to school or work on your favorite day?
   _____

7. Do you <u>ever</u> sleep in on your favorite day?
   _____

8. Do you <u>ever</u> take time-off on your favorite day?
   _____

EXERCISE 3:
Use your answers in Exercise 2 to write a paragraph that tells what you do on your favorite day.
Your first sentence should introduce your topic.

Start with: My favorite day is...   **Or**   On my favorite day I …

_____

_____

_____

_____

_____

Student Workbook

Lesson 15

EXERCISE 1: Make sentences by putting these words in the correct order. Remember to start each sentence with a capital letter and to put a period at the end.

1. beautiful, is, city, a, Victoria

2. live, Some, people, there, very, unfortunate

3. alcohol, Lonely, often, people, drink

4. help, often, Unfortunate, need, people.

5. doesn't, help, Alcohol, usually, people

6. in, cities, unfortunate, many, people, are, There, most

7. people, problems, often, have, Handicapped, many

8. job, They, can't, find, a

EXERCISE 2: MATCH THE MEANING

world

street people

handicapped people

drugs

dark

rich people

alcohol

problem

all the countries and waters
people take them to change the way they think
people who can't see, walk or talk well

what happens isn't good
they live on the streets
they have a lot of money

not much light
people drink it

Student Workbook   34

Lesson 15 Continued

EXERCISE 3: Answer in sentences

1. Are there many street people in your town?
   _____

2. Do street people have bad times?
   _____

3. What problem might a handicapped person have?
   _____

4. Do many people who aren't handicapped drink alcohol?
   _____

5. Do you think that alcohol helps people?
   _____

6. How do the street people often feel?
   _____

7. What will make someone's problems worse?
   _____

8. What do the street people need?
   _____

9. Do beautiful gardens help the street people?
   _____

10. We say, "The world walks by". What does that mean?
    _____

11. Where do most of the street people live?
    _____

12. Have you ever faced a bad problem?
    _____

Lesson 16

Answer in sentences

EXERCISE 1:

1. What do you think the name "The Open Door" means?
   _____
2. Who goes there?
   _____
3. Who gives bread to The Open Door?
   _____
4. Do volunteer workers do a lot of the work there?
   _____
5. Do you have a place like The Open Door in your city?
   _____
6. What do you think is the best about The Open Door?
   _____

EXERCISE 2:   **MATCH THE MEANING**

living room _____

newspaper _____

to volunteer _____

maybe _____

to bring _____

to sleep in _____

| you read it | to work for no money | to take something to a place |
| a comfortable place | perhaps | to stay in bed in the morning |

EXERCISE 3:

     comfortable   newspaper   street people   tea
     money   good   else   volunteer

In Victoria there is a place called The Open Door. It gives the _____ a warm and _____ place to go. When they are there, they can get a free cup of _____ or coffee and something to eat. They can also read a _____ and talk to their friends.

The people who do _____ work there don't want to be given any _____.

They feel _____ when they go home because they have helped someone _____.

Student Workbook

Lesson 16 Continued

ACTIVITY 5:

Divide into small groups.
Decide what Joe says to Bill and write it into your workbook.
They meet on a street in town, and decide to go to The Open Door.

Bill: Hi Joe! How are you doing?

Joe: _____

Bill: What are you doing this morning?

Joe: _____

Bill: Let's walk to The Open Door.
We can get a cup of coffee, it's cold today.

Joe: _____

Bill: I want to talk to someone. Maybe they can help me.

Joe: _____

Bill: My mother is sick and I have no money to get home.

Joe: _____

EXERCISE 4: Complete the sentences with tag questions, then answer the question.

If you don't know which verb to use in the question, think of the answer. It will help you.

1. The street people are often hungry, _____? _____.

2. The Open Door is a warm place, _____? _____.

3. Bill's mother is sick, _____? _____.

4. Bill wants to go home, _____? _____.

5. Someone can help Bill, _____? _____.

6. There are street people in your city, _____? _____.

7. Volunteer work makes you feel good, _____? _____.

8. Victoria has beautiful gardens, _____? _____.

Student Workbook 37

Lesson 17

EXERCISE 1:

Answer in sentences using contractions with <u>would</u> in your answers.

1. Would you want to work all night?
   _____

2. Would you order a salad with lettuce and tomatoes?
   _____

3. Would you like some tea?
   _____

4. Would you go out for dinner?
   _____

5. Would your cat eat a bird?
   _____

6. Would you want to have a cat?
   _____

7. Would your dog eat lettuce?
   _____

8. Would your friends want to play basketball?
   _____

9. Would you enjoy a crowded restaurant?
   _____

EXERCISE 2: Use the words below to complete the sentences.

wouldn't   it'd   a   she'd   for   in   he'd   they'd

Carol and her friends want to order something _____ a restaurant. Carol's friends can't speak English so Carol orders _____ them. Zula says _____ like the soup and salad. Berko says _____ like the pizza. Carol decides that _____ like the noodles. They agree that _____ all like a glass of juice.

The waiter said that the restaurant was crowded and _____ take a few minutes to make the orange juice. They all agreed that it _____ matter. It'd be okay.

Student Workbook   38

Lesson 17 Continued

EXERCISE 3:   MATCH THE MEANING

prefer   _____

tomato   _____

beverage   _____

patron   _____

ice cream   _____

lunchroom   _____

crowd   _____

menu   _____

to wish   _____

pineapple   _____

salad   _____

dessert   _____

a person who eats in a restaurant   what you like the best   it's very, very cold
a list of what you can order   a round red vegetable   you drink it
it has many cold vegetables   a lot of people   to want something
it's hot or cold and it's usually sweet   where you eat lunch   a kind of fruit

EXERCISE 4:   PRINT THE CORRECT WORDS UNDER THE PICTURES

_____   _____   _____

_____   _____   _____

Student Workbook   39

Lesson 18

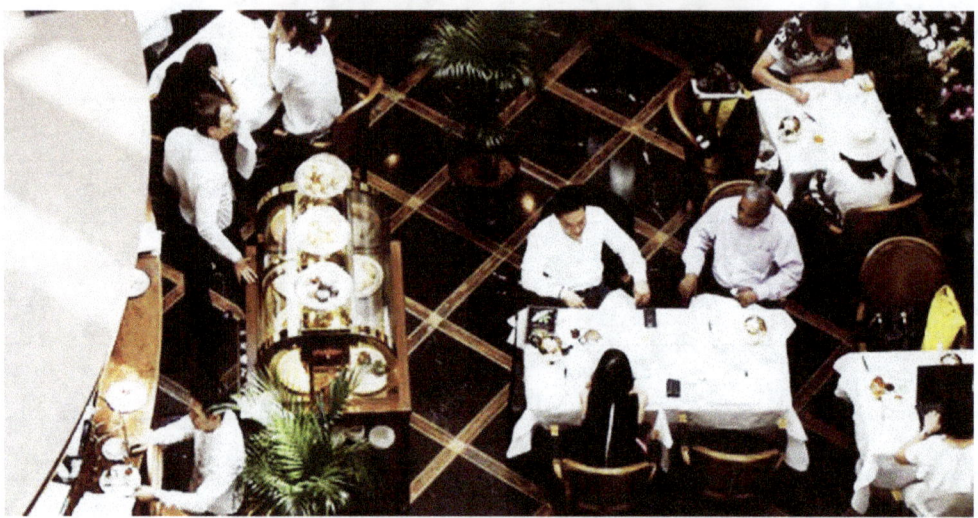

CHARLIE'S RESTAURANT
Noodles $3.95
Ice cream $1.50
Salad $2.25   Juice $.95
Soup $1.75   Tea $1.00

ACTIVITY 3:   **ASK YOUR PARTNER**   **USE REPORTED SPEECH**

EXAMPLE: Would you be interested in ordering mango juice?
_____ would be interested in ordering mango juice.

1. Would you like to live across from a restaurant?
   _____

2. Would you ask for pizza?
   _____

3. Would you wait for your friend at Charlie's?
   _____

4. Would you talk about Charlie's pizza with your friends?
   _____

5. Would you ask about Charlie's ice cream?
   _____

6. What kind of food are you interested in having?
   _____

7. Do the people in your country eat a lot of pizza?
   _____

Student Workbook   40

Lesson 18 Continued

EXERCISE 1: Complete the paragraphs below, using the prepositions from these phrases

to wait for	to arrive at	to ask for
to talk about	to be interested in	farther from…than
to read about	across from	stayed up
slept in	to pick up	competes in

Brian and Raymond are in a restaurant. Raymond is sitting across _____ Brian. They are waiting _____ Ruth and Pam. Brian has a hamburger and he asked _____ some coffee. He isn't as interested _____ Canadian food as Raymond. He is more interested _____ sports. He reads many books _____ sports and competes _____ many games.

The girls are late arriving _____ the restaurant. They stayed _____ late last night to study their English and so Pam slept _____ this morning. Then she had to pick ____ Ruth in her car. Ruth's hotel is farther _____ the restaurant _____ Pam's house.

EXERCISE 2: Answer these questions using the underlined phrase in the past tense.

1. Did you sleep in this morning?
   _____

2. Did you wait for your friend today?
   _____

3. Did you pick up a friend today?
   _____

4. Did you ask for help with your English?
   _____

5. Did you stay up late last night?
   _____

6. Did you talk about the latest movie?
   _____

7. Did you arrive at class on time?
   _____

8. Did you ask your friend for help?
   _____

9. Did you live across from a school last year?
   _____

Lesson 19

EXERCISE 1:   A contraction is often used with "have got".

Rewrite the following sentences using "have got" with a contraction.

She has blond hair.   She's got blond hair

1. They have a new house. _____
2. She has a big family. _____
3. We have some tea. _____
4. He has a hamburger. _____
5. I have a letter from my friend. _____
6. They have a soccer ball. _____
7. We have some English books. _____
8. The dog is happy. It has a bone. _____
9. The students are busy. They have work to do. _____

EXERCISE 2:   USING THE NEGATIVE:

Rewrite the following sentences using "have / has got" with a contraction and the negative.

NORTH AMERICAN	BRITISH	BRITISH NEGATIVE
She has blond hair.	She has got blond hair.	She hasn't got blond hair.
They have some money.	They have got some money.	They haven't got any money.

1. He doesn't have a car.
   _____

2. The picture doesn't have many people.
   _____

3. Three of the men don't have a bow.
   _____

4. They have no soccer ball.
   _____

5. They have no snow.
   _____

Student Workbook

42

Lesson 19 Continued

EXERCISE 3: USING HAVE / HAS GOT
Rewrite the following sentences using have / has got.

EXAMPLE: He has no tickets.   He hasn't got any tickets.

1. They have a new car. _____

2. Mexico City has no snow. _____

3. He needs to study. _____

4. They don't have any money. _____

5. She needs to get her hair cut. _____

6. The dogs have no home. _____

7. They have no time to wait. _____

8. He has something in his pocket. _____

9. The family has no food. _____

10. She has a small house. _____

EXERCISE 4:
Complete each sentence to show necessity.
    Use the following:

have / has to,   had to,   must

or   have / has got to (British form)

1. The man in front _____ pull.

2. Everyone _____

    help him.

3. The rope _____ not break.

4. They _____ be strong.

5. They _____ hold on to

    the rope.

Student Workbook   43

Lesson 20

JANE

JOHN

PETER

MIRANDA

John lives 1 kilometer from the school.
Jane lives 3 kilometers from the school.
Miranda lives 3 kilometers from the school.
Peter lives 5 kilometers from the school.

EXERCISE 1: Answer these questions in sentences using the above map.

1. How far from the school do you live?

   _____

2. Do you live farther from the school than Peter?

   _____

3. Who lives the closest to the school, John, Jane, Miranda or Peter?

   _____

4. Does Jane live as near to the school as John?

   _____

5. Who lives the same distance from the school as Miranda?

   _____

6. Would you want to live as far from your school as Peter?

   _____

7. Is the English School between Jane's house and Miranda's house?

   _____

Student Workbook

Lesson 20 Continued

EXERCISE 2: Complete the sentence with a tag question and then give the answer.

1. You came to English class today, _____? Yes,_____
2. Canada is a big country, _____? Yes,_____
3. You enjoy your holidays, _____? Yes,_____
4. You don't usually ride on an elephant, _____? No, _____
5. You aren't Canadian, _____? No, _____
6. You can't fly, _____? No, _____

EXERCISE 3: Put these words into sentences.

1. big, car, He, a red, has
   _____
2. liked, expensive, the, They, clothes, most, in, store, the
   _____
3. dress, wore, a, She, cotton, blue
   _____
4. black, Jim, his, rides, bicycle, always
   _____
5. usually, Mary, late, is
   _____
6. get, They, married, will, likely
   _____

EXERCISE 4: You may use these prepositions more than once to complete the sentences.

about   in   for   at   of   from

Sarah and Peter were meeting their friends Tom and Carol. They'd waited _____ fifteen minutes before the two friends finally arrived _____ the restaurant. Carol said that she'd slept _____ that morning and she was sorry. The four friends sat at a table across _____ each other and talked _____ the movie they saw last week.

They asked the waiter _____ some coffee. Then they all looked at the menu so they could decide what kind _____ dessert to order.

Student Workbook

HIGH BEGINNERS ESL LESSON PLANS BOOK 1 A CONVERSATIONAL APPROACH

TEACHER GUIDE

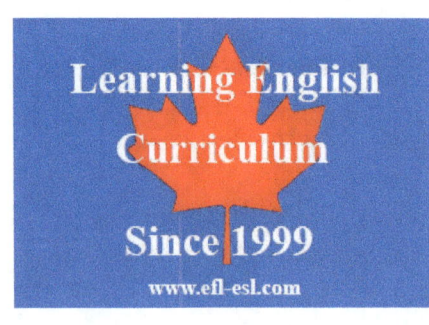

Daisy A. Stocker B.Ed., M.Ed.
George A Stocker D.D.S.

Lesson 1

ORAL QUESTIONS
REVIEW OF BOOK 1

To the teacher: This oral question review of Module1 includes the important grammatical points that were taught and stresses sentence word order.
The lesson numbers for the questions are listed with the sample questions.
If the students have difficulty with specific questions, then go to the listed lesson in the Teacher Guides of Beginners Book 1 or 2, to find more questions that teach the same grammatical point.
This review may also help you to identify any students who are not ready to continue with High Beginners Book 1. They should be able to answer about 80% of the questions.

Lesson 5

Is this your pen?	*Yes, it's my pen. / No, it isn't my pen.*
Whose book is this?	*It's his / her book.*

Lessons 9 and 10

Do you have a daughter?	*Yes, I have a daughter. / No, I don't have a daughter.*

Now go to another student and ask this question as you point to the student you just asked.

Does he / she have a daughter?	*Yes, he / she has a daughter.*
	No, he / she doesn't have a daughter.
Does your father come from Delhi?	*Yes, my father comes from Delhi.*
	No, my father doesn't come from Delhi.

Now go to another student and ask this question as you point to the student you just asked.

Does his / her father come from Delhi?	*Yes, his / her father comes from Delhi.*
	No, his / her father doesn't come from Delhi.

Lesson 11

How are you today?	*I'm fine thank you. (thanks)*
	Just great!
	I'm so-so. I'm okay.
	I'm not so good.

Lesson 13

Does she have two watches?	*Yes, she has two watches.*
	No, she doesn't have two watches./No, she doesn't have any...

Lesson 14

Do you have <u>some</u> juice?	*Yes, I have <u>some</u> juice.*
	No, I don't have <u>any</u> juice.
What is your surname?	*My surname is _____ .*

Teacher Guide

Lesson 1 Continued

Lesson 17

Who is in front of you?　　　　　　　　_____ *(name) is in front of me.*
　　　　　　　　　　　　　　　　　　The blackboard / door / a desk / is in front of me.
What is in your hand?　　　　　　　　*There is a _____ in my hand.*
　　　　　　　　　　　　　　　　　　There isn't anything in my hand.

Lesson 18

Where do you live? (with number)　　　*I live **at** (number) _____ street.*
Where do you live? (without number)　*I live **on** _____ street.*

Lesson 19

How many students are here?　　　　　*There are _____ students here.*
Is this book <u>yours</u>?　　　　　　　*Yes, it's <u>mine</u>. / No, it isn't <u>mine</u>.*

Lesson 21

Who is across from you?　　　　　　　_____ *is across from me.*
Do you have <u>some</u> matches?　　　*Yes, I have <u>some</u> matches.*
　　　　　　　　　　　　　　　　　　No, I don't have <u>any</u> matches.

Lesson 23

Can birds fly?　　　　　　　　　　　*Yes, birds can fly.*
Can you swim today?　　　　　　　　*Yes, I can swim today.*
　　　　　　　　　　　　　　　　　　No, I can't swim today.
Did you <u>phone</u> your friend last night?　*Yes, I <u>phoned</u> my friend last night.*
　　　　　　　　　　　　　　　　　　No, I <u>didn't phone</u> my friend last night.

Lesson 26

Did you <u>find</u> your friend?　　　　*Yes, I <u>found</u> my friend.*
　　　　　　　　　　　　　　　　　　No, I didn't find my friend.

Lesson 27

<u>Were</u> you at home last night?　　*Yes, I <u>was</u> at home last night.*
　　　　　　　　　　　　　　　　　　No, I <u>wasn't</u> at home last night.

Lesson 30 and 31

<u>Are</u> you <u>writing</u> a letter now?　*No, I'<u>m</u> not <u>writing</u> a letter now.*
Are you having a <u>day-off</u> work today?　*Yes, I'm having a <u>day-off</u> work today.*
　　　　　　　　　　　　　　　　　　No, I'm not having a <u>day-off</u> work today.

Teacher Guide

Lesson 1 Continued

Lesson 33

Were you wearing a hat this morning?

Yes, I was wearing a hat this morning.
No, I wasn't wearing a hat this morning.

Lesson 35

Will it rain tomorrow?

Yes, it will rain tomorrow.
No, it won't rain tomorrow.

Will you have some juice?

Yes, I'll have some juice please.
No, I won't have any juice, thanks.

Lesson 37

Are you going to see your friend today?

Yes, I'm going to see my friend today.
No, I'm not going to see my friend today.

Lesson 38

Do many people travel by plane?
Do you go to town on foot?

Yes, many people travel by plane.
Yes, I go to town on foot.
No, I don't go to town on foot.

PAGE 1 **ANSWERS TO THE WORKBOOK QUESTIONS** **EXERCISE 1:**

Ronald: *There is a good movie in town Silvia.*
Silvia: *I know.*
Ronald: *Can we go tonight?*
Silvia: *I can go on Saturday night.*
Ronald: *That is great!*
Silvia: *What time can we go?*
Ronald: *How about eight o'clock?*
Silvia: *That's great! Thanks Ronald.*

PAGE 1 **ANSWERS TO THE WORKBOOK QUESTIONS** **EXERCISE 2:**

time-off	*you don't have to work*
to note	*you want to remember it*
to love	*to like something / someone very much*
to think	*to have an idea about something*
a movie	*you watch it*
legs	*you walk with them*

Lesson 1 Continued

BINGO

DIRECTIONS: First, the students are to match the meaning by writing the number of the meanings in List 2 beside the words in List 1. EXAMPLE: 1. a nurse

Next, they are to write the <u>words</u> in List 1 into the BINGO squares. The words should be placed randomly so that all of the printed cards are different. The meanings in List 2 can then be called to begin playing the game as outlined below.

The teacher or a student can call the words in the WORDS TO CALL list, allowing the students time to find the matching word(s) among the ones that they have printed into the squares. Some help is given as the game is played, as the goal is for the students to learn the vocabulary.

For the first game, the students are to mark the matching word box with a small x in the top left-hand corner or use small objects such as a stones or beans for markers.
The winner(s) of the game call BINGO when they have a straight and complete row of **x** marked boxes. The marked rows can be in a straight vertical line, a straight horizontal line, or a straight diagonal line. The diagonal line must go from one corner to the other.

The FREE box is counted as a marked word when it is a part of the completed row. The game can be played a number of times until the students know the vocabulary well. For each successive game, use a different symbol to mark the boxes.

PAGE 2   ANSWERS TO THE WORKBOOK BINGO   ACTIVITY 4:

Note to the teacher: The students should write the words into the squares, <u>not the numbers</u>. If they put the numbers into the squares they won't learn the vocabulary.

MATCH THE MEANING

24	to start	9	morning	15	to travel	1	a nurse
4	legs	5	an actress	7	to tell	13	to leave
19	to know	21	to stay	10	will not	16	to visit
22	nearby	2	noon	8	to return	14	to give
11	clothes	20	to sleep	17	to laugh	23	to listen
6	notebook	12	time-off	18	to say	3	road

Teacher Guide

Lesson 2

ORAL QUESTIONS

What month is your birthday?	My birthday is **in** _____.
In what month is your national holiday?	Our national holiday is **in** _____.
	It's **in** _____.
What day of the month is your birthday?	My birthday is **on** ___ (month) ___ (number).
	It's **on** ___ (month) ___ (number).
What day is the first day of the year?	The first day of the year is **on** January 1st.
	It's **on** January 1st.
Were you born in March?	Yes, I was born **in** March.
	No, I wasn't born **in** March.
Is Christmas in December?	Yes, Christmas is **in** December.
What month is it now?	It's _____.
What day of the week is it?	It's _____.

Note to the teacher:
Questions that ask for a specific time may be answered with or without the AM or PM.
AM and PM are not used if the morning or afternoon is clear in the sentence.
For example, dinner wouldn't be eaten in the morning so the answer would be:
I ate dinner at 12:30 or perhaps at 6:00.
In spoken language AM and PM are seldom used.

What time did you eat dinner yesterday?	I ate dinner at _____.
What time did you come to class today?	I came to class at _____.
What time did you pick up your friend last night?	I picked up my friend at _____.
	I didn't pick up my friend.
	I'll go to bed at _____.
What time will you go to bed tonight?	
	I usually eat breakfast at _____.
What time do you usually eat breakfast?	I'll go home at _____.
When will you go home today?	Yes, my friend is younger than I am.
Is your friend younger than you are?	No, my friend isn't younger than I am. Yes, my friend is older than I am.
Is your friend older than you are?	No, my friend isn't older than I am.
	Yes, my cousin lives in town.
Does your cousin live in town?	No, my cousin doesn't live in town.
	Yes, there is a department store in my city.
Is there a department store in your city?	No, there isn't a department store in my city.
	Yes, I bought train tickets.
Did you buy train tickets?	No, I didn't buy train tickets.
	Yes, I have relatives in town.
Do you have relatives in town?	No, I don't have relatives in town.

Lesson 2 Continued

PAGE 3   ANSWERS TO THE WORKBOOK QUESTIONS   **EXERCISE 1:**

1. Who are Jim, Janet, Pam and Brian going to pick up?
   They are going to pick up Craig, Jessica, Ruth and Raymond.
2. How will Jim and his family get to the airport?
   They will go to the airport by car.
3. Who is Craig's brother?
   Jim is Craig's brother.
4. Who are Ruth and Raymond's cousins?
   Pam and Brian are their cousins.
5. Where are Ruth and Raymond from?
   They are from Melbourne, Australia.
6. Where are Ruth and Raymond going?
   They are going to Vancouver, Canada.
7. How will they travel from Melbourne to Sydney?
   They'll travel by bus.
8. How will they travel from Sydney to Vancouver?
   They'll travel by plane.
9. Where do Jim, Janet, Pam and Brian live?
   They live in Vancouver, Canada.
10. Who is younger than Raymond?
    Brian is younger than Raymond.
11. Who is older than Ruth?
    Pam is older than Ruth.

PAGE 4   ANSWERS TO THE WORKBOOK QUESTIONS   **ACTIVITY 4:**

1. What did you have for breakfast?   _____ had _____ for breakfast.

2. Did you come to class by motorcycle?   _____ came to class by motorcycle.
        _____ didn't come to class by motorcycle.

3. Do you go swimming in December?   _____ goes swimming in December.
        _____ doesn't go swimming in December.

4. Do you wear a coat in January?   _____ wears a coat in January.
        _____ doesn't wear a coat in January.

5. Do you have a holiday in July?   _____ has a holiday in July.
        _____ doesn't have a holiday in July.

6. Did you get time off-from work today?   _____ got time-off from work today.
        _____ didn't get time-off from work today.

7. Do you have a birthday in June?   _____ has a birthday in June.
        _____ doesn't have a birthday in June.

8. Were you born on December 31st?   _____ was born on December 31st.
        _____ wasn't born on December 31st.

Teacher Guide

Lesson 2 Continued

ACTIVITY 6: This is best done with the whole class.
Have the students sit in two rows (teams) facing each other.
Give each student some questions to ask members of the other row (team).

Did you visit your relatives during your holiday?
Yes, I visited my relatives during (my) (the) holiday.
No, I didn't visit my relatives during (my) (the) holiday.

Did you meet your friends at the airport?
Yes, I met my friends at the airport.
No, I didn't meet my friends at the airport.

Is your cousin younger than you are?
Yes, my cousin is younger than I am.
No, my cousin isn't younger than I am.

Did you buy tickets <u>for</u> a basketball game?
Yes, I bought tickets <u>for</u> a basketball game.
No, I didn't buy tickets <u>for</u> a basketball game.

Did you buy tickets <u>for</u> the bus to Sydney?
Yes, I bought tickets <u>for</u> the bus to Sydney.
No, I didn't buy tickets <u>for</u> the bus to Sydney.

Are you going to have some coffee for breakfast?
Yes, I am going to have some coffee for breakfast.
No, I'm not going to have any coffee for breakfast.

Are you going to have dinner tonight?
Yes, I'm going to have dinner tonight.
No, I'm not going to have dinner tonight.

Teacher Guide

Lesson 2 Continued

Are you going to pick up your friend in your car?
Yes, I'm going to pick up my friend in my car.
No, I'm not going to pick up my friend in my car.

How will you get to school tomorrow?
I'll get to school by car / bus / on foot.
I won't go to school tomorrow.

Who will you see at the movies next week?
I'll see my friend.
I won't see my friend.

What are you going to have for supper?
I'm going to have _____ for supper.

When will it be dinnertime?
It'll be dinnertime at _____.

Do you eat dinner at 12:15?
Yes, I eat dinner at 12:15.
No, I don't eat dinner at 12:15.

Do you get up at 7:00?
Yes, I get up at 7:00.
No, I don't get up at 7:00

Do you eat breakfast at half past seven?
Yes, I eat breakfast at half past seven.
No, I don't eat breakfast at 7:30.

Teacher Guide

Lesson 3

ORAL QUESTIONS

Do you sometimes wear blue jeans?	Yes, I sometimes wear blue jeans. No, I don't wear blue jeans.
You aren't wearing a dress, are you?	No, I'm not.
Do you work at night?	Yes, I work at night. No, I don't work at night.
Does an actress work in the theater?	Yes, an actress works in the theater.
You're not an actor, are you?	No, I'm not an actor.
Do you work in a department store?	Yes, I work in a department store. No, I don't work in a department store.
Do you like to laugh?	Yes, I like to laugh.
(Ask another student.)	
He / She likes to laugh, doesn't he / she?	Yes, he / she does.
Do you like to buy new clothes?	Yes, I like to buy new clothes. No, I don't like to buy new clothes.
He has a notebook, hasn't he?	Yes, he has.
Do you listen to music at night?	Yes, I listen to music at night. No, I don't listen to music at night.
What songs do you like the best?	I like _____ the best.
What cities do you like the best?	I like _____ the best.
You're not a nurse, are you?	No, I'm not. / Yes, I am.
You eat dinner at noon, don't you?	Yes, I do. No, I don't.
You wear shoes to school, don't you?	Yes, I do.
You didn't get time-off from work today, did you?	No, I didn't.

Note to the teacher: The verb "is" at the end of the sentence is grammatically correct but is not generally used. It is understood.

Are you younger than your friend (is)?	Yes, I'm younger than my friend (is). No, I'm not younger than my friend (is).
Are you older than your friend (is)?	Yes, I'm older than my friend (is). No, I'm not older than my friend (is).
Do you have relatives in town?	Yes, I have relatives in town. No, I don't have relatives in town.
Did you buy tickets for the bus?	Yes, I bought tickets for the bus. No, I didn't buy tickets for the bus.
Were you at home during the holidays?	Yes, I was at home during the holidays. No, I wasn't at home during the holidays.

Teacher Guide

Lesson 3 Continued

PAGE 5   **ANSWERS TO THE WORKBOOK QUESTIONS**   **EXERCISE 1:**

1. You were in English class, *weren't you*?   Yes, I was.
2. You can't ride a bicycle, *can you*?   No, I can't.
3. You have a home, *haven't you*?   Yes, I have.
4. She wasn't a student, *was she*?   No, she wasn't.
5. They aren't in town, *are they*?   No, they aren't.
6. It is cold today, *isn't it*?   Yes, it is. / No it isn't.
7. They can get a bus, *can't they*?   Yes, they can.
8. Flowers can grow, *can't they*?   Yes, they can.
9. India is a big country, *isn't it*?   Yes, it is.

PAGE 5   **ANSWERS TO THE WORKBOOK QUESTIONS,**   **EXERCISE 2:**

1. George lives here, *doesn't he*?   Yes, he does.
2. Dogs don't read, *do they*?   No, they don't.
3. They came here, *didn't they*?   Yes, they did.
4. You listen to music, *don't you*?   Yes, I do.
5. You don't sleep at noon, *do you*?   No, I don't.
6. We visited their friends, *didn't we*?   Yes, we did.

PAGE 6   **ANSWERS TO THE STUDENT READER QUESTIONS**   **ACTIVITY 3:**

You walked to class, *didn't you*? Yes, **I did**.   We come from Canada, *don't we*? **Yes, we do**.
No, **I didn't**.   No, we **don't**.
We study English, ***don't we***? Yes, **we do**.   We eat at noon, ***don't we***? **Yes, we do. No, we don't**.

PAGE 6   **ANSWERS TO THE WORKBOOKBOOK QUESTIONS**   **ACTIVITY 4:**

1. This isn't your birthday, *is it*?   No, it isn't.
2. You have a book, *haven't you*?   Yes, I have.
3. You're a student, *aren't you*?   Yes, I am.
4. You have a pen, *haven't you*?   Yes, I have.
5. You weren't born in 2000, *were you*?   No, I wasn't.
6. You can get a bus, *can't you*?   Yes, I can.
7. You like music, *don't you*?   Yes, I do.

PAGE 6   **ANSWERS TO THE WORKBOOK QUESTIONS**   **EXERCISE 3:**

1. *She is working in the mornings.*
2. *They meet at his house in the evenings.*
3. *They watched television at home last night.*
4. *She wrote in her notebook yesterday.*
5. *The dog followed them to school this morning.*
6. *Marietta has a beautiful dress, hasn't she?*
7. *Yes, she has.*

ACTIVITY 4:   Cut the questions on the next page into separate cards.
Divide the group into two teams. Give each student one or two question cards.
The students are to ask a student on the other team the question on their card(s).
All students should ask and answer at least one question.
Note: The most difficult questions are at the bottom half of the page.

Teacher Guide

Lesson 3 Continued

(name) _____ is here, isn't she? Answer: *Yes, she is.*

(name) _____ is a student, isn't she? **Answer:** *Yes, she is.*

(name) _____ isn't here, is he? Answer: *No, he isn't.*

It isn't cold, is it?
Answer: *No, it isn't.*

There isn't a class on Sunday, is there?
Answer: *No, there isn't.*

You aren't playing football now, are you?
Answer: *No, I'm not.*

There wasn't a class on Saturday, was there?
Answer: *No, there wasn't.*

You don't eat breakfast at night, do you?
Answer: *No, I don't.*

There are some students here, aren't there?
Answer: *Yes, there are.*

Some men play soccer, don't they? **Answer:** *Yes, they do.*

You study English, don't you?
Answer: *Yes, I do.*

(name) _____ has a watch, hasn't he?
Answer: *Yes, he has.*

(name) _____ is a teacher, isn't he / she?
Answer: *Yes, he / she is.*

That book is yours, isn't it?
Answer: *Yes, it is.*

Those aren't your pens, are they? **Answer:** *No, they aren't.*

It's hot today, isn't it?
Answer: *Yes, it is.*

You can't go to a restaurant now, can you?
Answer: *No, I can't.*

It rains sometimes, doesn't it?
Answer: *Yes, it does.*

You like eating in a restaurant, don't you?
Answer: *Yes, I do.*

They grow coffee in Brazil, don't they?
Answer: *Yes, they do.*

Some girls like beautiful clothes, don't they?
Answer: *Yes, they do.*

There are trains in this country, aren't there?
Answer: *Yes, there are.*

Teacher Guide

Lesson 4   Review

Note to the teacher: Re - Page 7 of the Student Reader:

3.   *This* big car is nearer. It is grammatically correct to say "This big car is nearer." because there are only two cars.
    However, in common usage we often say: "This big car is the nearest."

ORAL QUESTIONS

Do you have a cousin?	Yes, I have a cousin.
	No, I don't have a cousin.
Paul was born in 1994. How old is he?	He is _____ years old.
What time do you have breakfast?	I have breakfast at _____ (o'clock). Yes,
Did you talk about the soccer game yesterday?	I talked about the soccer game yesterday. No, I didn't talk about the soccer game... Yes, my
Is your friend older than you are?	friend is older than I am.
	No, my friend isn't older than I am.
You're wearing blue jeans, aren't you?	Yes, I am.
Did you remember to bring your book to class?	Yes, I remembered to bring my book to class.
	No, I didn't remember to bring my book to...
Can you run?	Yes, I can run.
Do flowers grow?	Yes, flowers grow.

PAGE 8   WORKBOOK ROLE CARDS   ACTIVITY 1:

Give one name to each student.

Miranda Bates July 25, 2001	Michael Ashton April 3, 2005	Linda Watts July 22, 2000	Allan Dunning May 19, 2006	Marie McLaren June 30, 2003
Joseph Woods April 15, 1999	Elizabeth Fraser June 28, 2004	Tom Skala August 12, 1997	Samuel Munn March 10, 2002	Anne Rhodes May 14, 1996
Sally Ray October 15, 1998	Daniela Black May 11, 1998	Brian Vernon April 17, 1997	Marg Selkirk April 2, 2001	Bob Wright March 1, 1995

PAGE 7   ANSWERS TO THE WORKBOOK QUESTIONS   EXERCISE 1:

1. *That* small car is far away.   3.   *This* big car is nearer.
2. *These* three birds are near.   4.   *Those* two birds are farther away.

Teacher Guide

Lesson 4 Continued

PAGE 7 ANSWERS TO THE WORKBOOK QUESTIONS **EXERCISE 2:**

1. The big car is near us, *isn't it?* Yes, it is.
2. The three birds are near the big car, *aren't they?* Yes, they are.
3. There are three birds near us, *aren't there?* Yes, there are.
4. The small car isn't near us, *is it?* No, it isn't.
5. There is one small car, *isn't there?* Yes, there is.

PAGE 7,8 ANSWERS TO THE WORKBOOK QUESTIONS **EXERCISE 3:**

1. The boats are in the water, *aren't they?* Yes, they are.
2. The boats aren't near the elephants, *are they?* No, they aren't. Yes, he is.
3. The old man is beside the bicycle, *isn't he?*
4. The girl is on the bicycle, *isn't she* Yes, she is.
5. The girl can ride the bicycle, *can't she?* Yes, she can.
6. The man is close to the lady, *isn't he?* Yes, he is.
7. The man is beside the lady, *isn't he?* Yes, he is.
8. They are dressed formally, *aren't they?* Yes, they are.
9. The elephants aren't in the water, *are they?* No, they aren't. No, they can't.
10. The elephants can't ride a bicycle, *can they?*
11. They aren't black, *are they?* No, they aren't.

PAGE 8 ANSWERS TO THE WORKBOOK QUESTIONS **EXERCISE 4:**

1. Do you live far from here? *Yes, I live far from here.*
   No, I don't live far from here.
2. Did you get time-off from work last week? *Yes, I got time-off from work last week. No, I didn't get time off from work last week. Yes, I love to buy new clothes.*
3. Do you love to buy new clothes?
   No, I don't love to buy new clothes.
4. Which movie did you like the best? *I liked _____ the best.*
5. Are you going to listen to music today? *Yes, I'm going to listen to music today. No, I'm not going to listen to music today.*

TEST 1

PAGE 15 ANSWERS TO THE TEST QUESTIONS TEST 1:

1. What month was Ronald born? — *He was born in June.*
2. What day was he born? — *He was born on June 8th.*
3. How old is Ronald? — *Ronald is _____.*
4. hot, summer, It, in, is, the — *It is hot in the summer.*
5. music, listen, students, to, The — *The students listen to music.*
6. got, work, They, from, time-off — *They got time-off from work.*
7. friend, picked up, She, her — *She picked up her friend.*

8. You have a pen, *haven't you (don't you)*?
9. **Answer:** *Yes, I have (I do).*
10. Elephants are big, *aren't they*?
11. **Answer:** *Yes, they are.*
12. You eat breakfast in the morning, *don't you*?
13. **Answer:** *Yes, I do. / No, I don't.*

14. Do you go to bed at 10:00 PM? — *Yes, I go to bed at 10:00 PM.*
    No, I don't go to bed at 10:00 PM.
15. Are you wearing blue jeans today? — *Yes, I'm wearing blue jeans today.*
    No, I'm not wearing blue jeans today.

16. They were *at* home *in* the morning.

Teacher Guide

TEST 1   LESSONS 1 TO 4

NAME: _____   **Answer in sentences.** (4 marks each)

1. What month was Ronald born?
   _____

2. What day was he born?
   _____

3. How old is Ronald?
   _____

RONALD
JUNE 8, 1998

Put these words into sentences. (4 marks each)

4. hot, summer, It, in, is, the
   _____

5. music, listen, students, to, The
   _____

6. got, work, They, from, time-off,
   _____

7. friend, picked up, She, her
   _____

Complete the tag question and answer it. (2 marks each)

8. You have a pen, _____ _____

9. **Answer:** _____ _____ _____ .

10. Elephants are big, _____ _____?

11. **Answer:** _____ _____ _____ .

12. You eat breakfast in the morning, _____ _____?

13. **Answer:** _____ _____ _____ .

Answer these questions in sentences. (4 marks each)

14. Do you go to bed at 10:00 PM.?
    _____

15. Are you wearing blue jeans today?
    _____

Use prepositions to complete the sentence. (1 mark each)

16. They were _____ home _____ the morning.

Teacher Guide   15

Lesson 5
ORAL QUESTIONS

To the teacher:

Ask one student – "How far from the school do you live?"
Write their answer on the blackboard as shown below.
Ask other students until you find one that lives a different distance from the school.
Write their answer on the blackboard under the first one.
Ask two more students who live different distances from the school.
Write their answers on the blackboard under the others.
Finally, find a student that lives the same distance from the school as any one of the others.
Write their answer on the blackboard under the first one.

EXAMPLE:
_____ lives _____ kilometers from the school.
_____ lives _____ kilometers from the school.
_____ lives _____ kilometers from the school.
_____ lives _____ kilometers from the school.
_____ lives _____ kilometers from the school.
This last one will be the same distance as one of the others.

Now ask the students these questions.
Who lives the closest to the school?
Who lives the farthest from the school?
Who lives farther from the school than _____?
Who lives closer to the school than _____?
Who lives the same distance from the school as _____?

Do you live farther from the school than _____?
Do you live nearer to the school than _____?
Do you live near to _____?
Do you live the same distance from the school as _____?
Do you live as far from the school as _____?
Do you live as close to the school as _____?

The teacher could ask the students a number of questions about the location of where they live. This would provide practice in making distance comparisons.

The following are some typical questions and answers.
1. Which is farther from here, the Post Office, or the bus stop?
   The _____ is farther from here.
2. Which is the farthest from here, London, Rome or Bombay?
   _____ is the farthest from here.
3. Which is the closest to our town, New York, Rome or Delhi?
   _____ is the closest.
4. Is London closer to Paris than Delhi?
   Yes, London is closer to Paris than Delhi.

Teacher Guide

Lesson 5 Continued

PAGE 9   **ANSWERS TO THE WORKBOOK QUESTIONS**   **EXERCISE 1:**

1. *Melanie lives one kilometer from the English School.*
2. *Jim lives ten kilometers from the English School.*
3. *Melanie lives nearer to the English School than John.*
4. *Pamela lives as far from the English School as John.*
   John lives as far from the English School as Pamela.
5. *Jim lives the farthest from the English School.*

PAGE 10   **ANSWERS TO THE WORKBOOK QUESTIONS**   **EXERCISE 2:**

1. *Melanie lives closer to the English School than Pamela.*
2. *Jim lives farther from the English School than John.*
3. *Pamela lives the same distance from the English School as John.*
4. *Melanie lives the closest to the English School.*
5. *_____ lives the same distance from the English School as me.*
6. *Yes, I live farther from the English School than Jim.*
   No, I don't live farther from the English School than Jim.
7. *Yes, I live closer to the English School than Melanie.*
   No, I don't live closer to the English School than Melanie.
8. *Yes, I live the same distance from the English School as Pamela. No, I don't live the same distance from the English School as Pamela.*
9. *Yes, I live as close to the English School as Melanie.*
   No, I don't live as close to the English School as Melanie.
10. *Yes, I live farther from the English School than Pamela.*
    No, I don't live farther from the English School than Pamela.

PAGE 11   **ANSWERS TO THE BINGO**   **ACTIVITY 4:**

10 the day after Tuesday	16 you don't work	11 food in the morning	24 this day
17 works in a school	5 the last month	14 where a plane goes	15 not as old as
20 half past ten	22 you listen to it	23 a big animal	12 you wear them
2 to come back	4 bigger than	18 Saturday and Sunday	13 not young
1 next to	21 played with a ball	8 doctors work there	7 half past two
19 the next day	6 not far	9 day after Wednesday	3 you ride it

Lesson 6

Note to the teacher:
In some questions and answers the verb at the end is understood and often not spoken.
For example: Are you younger than your friend <u>is</u>? (grammatically correct)
We would likely say: Are you younger than your friend? (common usage)

The use of "young<u>er</u>" and "<u>the</u> young<u>est</u>"

Grammatically correct: Who is younger? (because there are only two.)
Common usage: Who is the youngest? (Grammatically this superlative should be used with three or more items.)

ORAL QUESTIONS

What city is a good place to live?	_____ is a good place to live.
Which is the biggest city in your country?	_____ is the biggest city.
Which is better for you, pop or juice?	Juice is better for me.
	Pop is better for me.

Note to the teacher: "Which is better for you" means which is better for your health.

Is your friend older than you (are)?	Yes, my friend is older than me (I am).
	No, I am older than my friend(is). Yes, I
Are you younger than your friend (is)?	am younger than my friend(is). No, I
	am not younger than my friend(is).
What is the best car in your country?	_____ is the best car in my country.
Are you interested in clothes?	Yes, I'm interested in clothes.
	No, I'm not interested in clothes.
Do you have some of books?	Yes, I have some of books.
	No, I don't have any books.
Do you like soccer better than basketball?	Yes, I like soccer better than basketball. I
What drink do you like the best?	like _____ the best.
What is made in our town?	_____ is (are) made in our town.
Are our winters warmer than Canadian winters?	Yes, our winters are warmer than Canadian winters.
	No, our winters aren't warmer than…
Are soccer games exciting?	Yes, soccer games are exciting.
	No, soccer games aren't exciting.
Do you like soccer better than archery?	Yes, I like soccer better than archery. No, I don't like soccer better than… Yes, it's
Is it your birthday today?	my birthday today.
	No, it isn't my birthday today.
What is the most exciting, archery, basketball or soccer?	_____ is the most exciting.

PAGE 12   ANSWERS TO THE WORKBOOK QUESTIONS   EXERCISE 1:

Raymond: I hear you have a new department store here. What ***is it like***? I'm
Ruth: interested in ***clothes***.
Ruth: You have hot summers, ***don't you***?
Raymond: Our winters ***aren't as cold as yours*** / ***aren't very cold***.

Teacher Guide

Lesson 6 Continued

PAGE 12 **ANSWERS TO THE WORKBOOK QUESTIONS** **ACTIVITY 5:**

1. **Do you like soccer <u>more than</u> basketball?**
   _____ likes soccer more than basketball.
   _____ likes basketball more than soccer.
2. **Do you like hiking <u>more than</u> swimming?**
   _____ likes hiking more than swimming.
   _____ likes swimming more than hiking.
3. **What do you think is <u>the best</u>, sports, reading or music?**_____
   thinks _____ is the best.
4. **What are you <u>the most</u> interested in?**
   _____ is the most interested in _____.
5. **Do you think that cold weather is <u>better than</u> hot weather?**
   Yes,_____ thinks that cold weather is better than hot weather. No,
   _____doesn't think that cold weather is better than hot weather.
6. **What do you do <u>the most</u> often, read, hike or watch TV?**_____
   reads/hikes/watches TV/ the most often.

PAGE 13 **ANSWERS TO THE WORKBOOK QUESTIONS** **EXERCISE 2:**

1. What city are Ruth and Raymond from? — They are from Melbourne.
2. Does India have <u>more</u> people <u>than</u> Canada? — Yes, India *has more people than Canada.*
3. Which country has <u>the most</u> people, Australia, India or Canada? (India) — *India has the most people.*
4. Are many people in your country <u>interested in</u> soccer? — *Yes, many people are interested in soccer. No, not many people are interested...* Yes, *women are more interested in clothes*
5. Are women <u>more</u> interested in clothes <u>than</u> men? — *than men.* *No, women aren't more interested in clothes.*
6. Are International games <u>more</u> exciting <u>than</u> home team games? — *Yes, international games are more exciting than home team games. No, international games aren't more... I'm*
7. What sports are you <u>interested in</u>? — *interested in _____.*

PAGE 13 **ANSWERS TO THE WORKBOOK QUESTIONS** **EXERCISE 3:**

department store	*a store that sells many things – food, clothes etc.*
international	*all the countries of the world*
birthday	*the day you were born*
sports	*activities like soccer, swimming, archery etc.*
winter	*cold time of year*
summer	*the hot time of year*
weather	*rain, snow, sun etc.*
close to	*near to*
etcetra = etc.	*it means more of the same kind of things*
sun	*it keeps us warm*

Teacher Guide   19

Lesson 7

ORAL QUESTIONS

Which is more expensive, a bicycle or a car?
Who is the tallest in this class?
Am I the shortest in this class?

Is a bicycle faster than walking?

A car is more expensive. _____ is the tallest in this class. Yes, you are the shortest in this class. No, you aren't the shortest in this class. Yes, a bicycle is faster than walking.

Is a plane faster than a motorcycle?
Can you run faster than a train?
Is walking slower than a bus?
Is a truck heavier than a car?

Yes, a plane is faster than a motorcycle.
No, I can't run faster than a train.
Yes, walking is slower than a bus.
Yes, a truck is heavier than a car.

Are bicycles lighter than buses?
Who came to class the earliest?
Who came to class the latest?
Who came to class later than you did?

Yes, bicycles are lighter than buses.
_____ came to class the earliest.
_____ came to class the latest.
_____ came to class later than I did.

Is this desk wider than that one?

Yes, this desk is wider than that one. No, it is narrower than that one.
It is the same width as that one.

Is this desk narrower than that one?

Yes, this desk is narrower than that one.
No, it is wider than that one.
It is the same width as that one.

Did you come to class later than _____?

Who came to class earlier than _____?

Are you taller than your mother (is)?

Yes, I came to class later than _____.
No, I came to class earlier than _____.
_____ came to class earlier than _____.
Yes, I am taller than my mother (is). No, I'm not taller than my mother (is).

Are you shorter than your friend (is)?

Are very good clothes the most expensive?

Do you have a few pencils? (**Note- a few = 2 +**)

Yes, I am shorter than my friend (is). No, I am taller than my friend (is). Yes, very good clothes are the most expensive.
Yes, I have a few pencils.
No, I don't have a few pencils.
No, I have one pencil.

Do you have a small dog?

Yes, I have a small dog.
No, I have a big dog.
No, I don't have a dog.

Are you interested in cars?

Yes, I'm interested in cars.
No, I'm not interested in cars.

Lesson 7 Continued

PAGE 13   ANSWERS TO THE STUDENT READER QUESTIONS   ACTIVITY 1:

1. No, they weren't expensive.
2. Yes, it was better than the big one.
3. Yes, the smallest store has the most expensive clothes.
4. Raymond has a bicycle.
5. Yes, Brian can go faster than Raymond.
6. Brian's father can go the fastest.

PAGE 14   ANSWERS TO THE WORKBOOK QUESTIONS   EXERCISE 1:

1. The big store had the cheapest clothes.
2. The smallest store had the most expensive clothes.
3. No, the cheap clothes weren't the best.
4. No, the smallest store didn't have the cheapest clothes.
5. Yes, the beautiful clothes were more expensive than the cheap clothes.
6. No, I don't think that the cheapest clothes are the best.
   Yes, I think that the cheapest…

7. Brian's father can go the fastest.
8. No, Brian can't go faster than his father can.
9. No, Raymond can't go faster than Brian can.
10. Raymond goes the slowest.
11. Yes, Raymond goes slower than Brian's father does.
12. No, a bicycle can't go as fast as a car.
13. I want to have a _____.

PAGE 15   ANSWERS TO THE WORKBOOK QUESTIONS   EXERCISE 2:

The boys didn't go shopping **_for_** clothes.
They talked **_about_** things that boys are **_interested_** in.
Raymond has a bicycle. He can't go very **_fast_**.
Brian has a motorcycle. It can go **_faster than_** Raymond's bicycle.
Brian's father has a Mercedes sports car. He can go **_the fastest_**.

PAGE 15   ANSWERS TO THE WORKBOOK QUESTIONS   ACTIVITY 5:

1. _____ lives **_closer to_** / **_farther from_** the school than I do.
2. _____ got to class **_earlier than_** / **_later than_** I did.
3. _____ **_is taller than_** I am. / _____ **_is not as tall as_** I am.
4. _____ **_is shorter than_** I am. / _____ **_is not as short as_** I am.

PAGE 15   ANSWERS TO THE WORKBOOK QUESTIONS   EXERCISE 3:

1. Yes, today is **_hotter than_** yesterday.
   No, today isn't **_hotter than_** yesterday.
2. A car is **_not bigger than_** a train.
   A car **_isn't bigger than_** a train.
3. An **_airplane_** goes **_the fastest_**.
4. A **_car_** is **_the most expensive_**.
5. A **_pencil_** is **_the least expensive_**.

Teacher Guide

Lesson 7 Continued

ACTIVITY 6: Cut these questions into cards and give one or two cards to each student.
Divide the students into two teams.
The students are to ask their question(s) to someone on the other team.
Each student should ask and answer at least one question.
A team gets one point for each correct answer.

Are you shorter than your friend is?
Yes, I'm shorter than my friend is. No, I'm not shorter than my friend is.

Do you have a small dog?
Yes, I have a small dog.
No, I don't have a small dog.

Are you the tallest in this class? *Yes, I'm the tallest in this class.*
No, I'm not the tallest in this class.

Who has the least books?
_____ has the least books.

Is this the widest desk in this room?
Yes, it's the widest desk in this room.
No, it isn't the widest desk in this room.

What car is the most expensive?
A _____ is the most expensive.

Is a bicycle slower than a train? *Yes, a bicycle is slower than a train.*

Are people lighter than elephants?
Yes, people are lighter than elephants.

Were you late coming to class today?
Yes, I was late coming to class today.
No, I wasn't late coming to class today.

Are there fewer students here today than yesterday?
Yes, there are fewer students here today than... No, there aren't fewer students here today than... No, there are more students here today than...

Are boys more interested in cars than girls are?
Yes, boys are more interested in cars than girls are.
No, boys aren't more interested in cars than girls...

Is a car heavier than a bicycle?
Yes, a car is heavier than a bicycle.

Do you have a few pens?
Yes, I have a few pens.
No, I don't have any pens.

Is a hamburger cheaper than a bicycle?
Yes, a hamburger is cheaper than a bicycle.

Did you get to class earlier than the others did?
Yes, I got to class earlier than the others did. No, I didn't get to class earlier than the others did.

Do you like motorcycles better than cars?
Yes, I like motorcycles better than cars.
No, I don't like motorcycles better than...

Teacher Guide

Lesson 8   Review

Note to the teacher: Some vocabulary is introduced in many of the review lessons.
This is intended to help the students by spreading the learning of the words over a greater period of time. For the most part these new words aren't used on the test given with the same lesson.
If some students find this to be a problem, they can look ahead in their textbooks the week before the review lesson in order to study the new words.

TEACHER'S REFERENCE

> If a one-syllable word ends with a single consonant, we usually double the final consonant before adding an ending that begins with a vowel.
>
> **EXAMPLES:**   thin - thinner   sad - sadder
>   big – bigger   tan - tanned
>   stop - stopped   cut - cutter
>   wet - wetter   hot – hotter
>
> **The vowels in these words sound as in the following:**
>
> a - cat   e - pet   i - it   o - on   u - cup

ORAL QUESTIONS

Which is better for you, pop or juice? *Juice is better for me.*
Pop is better for me.

Are you taller than your mother is? *Yes, I am taller than my mother is.*
No, I'm not taller than my mother is. Yes, I

Are you shorter than your friend is? *am shorter than my friend is.*
No, I am taller than my friend is.

Is this book wider than that one? *Yes, it is wider than that one.*
No, it isn't wider than that one.
No, it is narrower than that one.

Can you run faster than a train? *No, I can't run faster than a train.*

What is better than travelling by train? What is the best way to travel? What food is better than a hamburger? What is the best food?
Travelling by car / plane / boat is better.
Travelling by ___ is the best way to travel.
_____ is better than a hamburger.
_____ is the best food.

Do you have some books?
Who has more books than _____?
Who has the most books?
Are you interested in airplanes?

Yes, I have some books. _____
has more books _____.
_____ has the most books.
Yes, I'm interested in airplanes.
No, I'm not interested in airplanes.

Did you get married last year? *Yes, I got married last year.*
No, I didn't get married last year.

Lesson 8 Continued

PAGE 16   ANSWERS TO THE WORKBOOK QUESTIONS   EXERCISE 1:

1. *Traveling* by plane is _____.
2. *Traveling* by train is _____.
3. *Traveling* by bicycle is _____.
4. *Eating* a hot dog is _____.
5. *Drinking* a lot of cold pop is _____.
6. *Driving* a motorcycle is _____.
7. *Skiing* to class is _____.

PAGE 16   ANSWERS TO THE WORKBOOK QUESTIONS   EXERCISE 2:

1. Did you come to class **earlier than** your friend did?
2. Are you **hungrier than** you were this morning?
3. Are you **taller than** your friend is?
4. Are you **the youngest** in your family?
5. Walking is **the slowest** way to travel.
7. Russia is **the biggest** country.
8. A train is **heavier than** a bicycle.
9. Skiing is **faster than** walking.

PAGE 17   ANSWERS TO THE WORKBOOK QUESTIONS   ACTIVITY 2:

1. __ lives __ kilometer(s) from the school.

2. Yes, __ lives farther from the school than I do. No, __ doesn't live farther from the school than I do.

3. Yes, __ lives nearer to the school than I do.
   No, __ doesn't live nearer to the school than I do.

4. _____ lives the farthest from the school.

5. _____ lives the nearest to the school.

6. Yes, the school is close to _____'s home.
   No, the school isn't close to _____'s home.

7. A _____ is closer to _____'s home.

8. Yes,____ is as tall as his/her father.
   No,_____ isn't as tall as his/her father.

9. Yes, _____ is taller than I am. No, _____ isn't taller than I am.

10. Yes, _____ is the shortest.
    No, _____ isn't the shortest.

11. Yes, ___ has more books than I do. No, _ doesn't have more books than…

12. _____ has the most books.

13. Yes,___'s town is as big as New York.
    No,___'s town isn't as big as New York.

PAGE 18   ANSWERS TO THE BINGO   ACTIVITY 3:

1	weekend	Saturday and Sunday	13 time-off	weekdays *you don't work*
2	hot	opposite of cold	14 slow	not fast
3	birthday	The day you were born.	15 the least	the fewest
4	clothes	you wear them	16 expensive	something is a lot of money.
5	neighbors	They live near you. not	17 evening	7:00 to 11:00 PM
6	a few	many	18 tomorrow	the next day
7	far	a long way off	19 early	opposite of late
8	many	a lot	20 narrow	opposite of wide
9	cousin	your relative opposite of	21 month	thirty (one) days
10	big	small	22 Canada	a country
11	noon	12:00	23 late	opposite of early
12	week	It has seven days	24 tall	opposite of short

Teacher Guide

TEST 2   LESSONS 5 TO 8

NAME: _____ **Answer the oral questions in sentences.** (4 marks each)

1. _____

2. _____

3. _____

4. _____

5. _____

Answer these questions in sentences. (4 marks each)

6. Does your country have a lot of soccer teams? (yes or no)

   _____

7. Are you taller than your friend?

   _____

8. Do you get more rain in July than in January?

   _____

9. What is the most expensive, a pen, a bicycle or a plane?

   _____

10. Is a man heavier than a car?

    _____

Write the correct meaning beside each word. (2 marks each)

weekend _____   the fewest _____

birthday _____   neighbors _____

noon _____

MEANINGS:

the day you were born   the least
12:00   Saturday and Sunday
you live near them

Teacher Guide

Lesson 8 Continued

QUESTIONS AND ANSWERS TO THE ORAL QUESTIONS FOR TEST 2

1. **Do you live more than one kilometer from this school?**
   Yes, I live more than one kilometer from this school. No, I don't live more than one kilometer from this school.
2. **Do you live closer to this school than your friend?** *Yes, I live closer to this school than my friend.*
   No, I don't live closer to this school than my friend.
3. **Can a bicycle go faster than a car?**
   No, a bicycle can't go faster than a car.
4. **Do you drink a lot of juice?**
   Yes, I drink a lot of juice.
   No, I don't drink a lot of juice.
5. **Are you interested in learning English?**
   Yes, I'm interested in learning English.
   No, I'm not interested in learning English.

ANSWERS TO THE WRITTEN TEST QUESTIONS

6. **Does your country have a lot of soccer teams?**
   Yes, my country has a lot of soccer teams.
   No, my country doesn't have a lot of soccer teams.
7. **Are you taller than your friend?**
   Yes, I'm taller than my friend.
   No, I'm not taller than my friend.
8. **Do you get more rain in July than in January?**
   Yes, we get more rain in July than in January.
   No, we don't get more rain in July than in January.
9. **What is the most expensive, a pen, a bicycle or a plane?** *A plane is the most expensive.*
10. **Is a man heavier than a car?**
    No, a man isn't heavier than a car.

Write the correct meaning beside the word. (2 marks each)

weekend	*Saturday and Sunday*	the fewest	*the least*
birthday	*the day you were born*	neighbors	*you live near them*
noon	*12:00*		

Teacher Guide

Lesson 9

ORAL QUESTIONS

Do you swim?
　　　　　　　　　　　　　　　　　　　　Yes, I swim.
　　　　　　　　　　　　　　　　　　　　No, I don't swim.

Do you go to a lake?
　　　　　　　　　　　　　　　　　　　　Yes, I go to a lake.
　　　　　　　　　　　　　　　　　　　　No, I don't go to a lake.

Do you like to hike in the mountains?
　　　　　　　　　　　　　　　　　　　　Yes, I like to hike in the mountains.
　　　　　　　　　　　　　　　　　　　　No, I don't like to hike in the mountains.

Do you think that dogs are stupid?
　　　　　　　　　　　　　　　　　　　　Yes, I think that dogs are stupid.
　　　　　　　　　　　　　　　　　　　　No, I don't think that dogs are stupid.

Are there some mountains in Canada?
　　　　　　　　　　　　　　　　　　　　Yes, there are some mountains in Canada.

Is it very warm in February in Australia?
　　　　　　　　　　　　　　　　　　　　Yes, it's very warm in February in Australia. No, the temperature is perfect in February…

Did you decide to go to a lake last Sunday?
　　　　　　　　　　　　　　　　　　　　Yes, I decided to go to a lake last Sunday.
　　　　　　　　　　　　　　　　　　　　No, I didn't decide to go to lake last…

Do you think that juice is terrible?
　　　　　　　　　　　　　　　　　　　　Yes, I think that juice is terrible.
　　　　　　　　　　　　　　　　　　　　No, I don't think that juice is terrible.

Lakes are wonderful, aren't they?
　　　　　　　　　　　　　　　　　　　　Yes, they are.

She's beautiful, isn't she?
　　　　　　　　　　　　　　　　　　　　Yes, she's beautiful./ Yes, she is.

Is _____ a fast worker?
　　　　　　　　　　　　　　　　　　　　Yes, _____ is a fast worker.
　　　　　　　　　　　　　　　　　　　　No, _____ isn't a fast worker.

Is a horse faster than a train?
　　　　　　　　　　　　　　　　　　　　No, a horse isn't faster than a train.

Does your friend work faster than you? Is
　　　　　　　　　　　　　　　　　　　　Yes, my friend works faster than I do (me).
　　　　　　　　　　　　　　　　　　　　No, my friend doesn't work faster than I do (me).

your friend taller than you are?
　　　　　　　　　　　　　　　　　　　　Yes, my friend is taller than I am.
　　　　　　　　　　　　　　　　　　　　No, my friend is shorter than I am.
　　　　　　　　　　　　　　　　　　　　No, my friend isn't taller than I am.

Are you interested in English?
　　　　　　　　　　　　　　　　　　　　Yes, I'm interested in English
　　　　　　　　　　　　　　　　　　　　No, I'm not interested in English.

Which is farther from here, New York or Delhi?
　　　　　　　　　　　　　　　　　　　　_____ is farther from here.

Are chicken sandwiches better than cheese sandwiches?
　　　　　　　　　　　　　　　　　　　　Yes, chicken sandwiches are better than cheese…
　　　　　　　　　　　　　　　　　　　　No, chicken sandwiches aren't better than…

Do you think the water at the lake is too cold?
　　　　　　　　　　　　　　　　　　　　Yes, I think the water at the lake is too cold. No, I don't think the water at the lake is too…

Teacher Guide

Lesson 9 Continued

PAGE 19   **ANSWERS TO THE WORKBOOK QUESTIONS**   **EXERCISE 1:**
1. Pam, Brian, Raymond and Ruth went to the lake.
2. No, Brian doesn't think that Toto is a smart dog. / He thinks Toto is stupid.
3. They took cheese and pickle sandwiches and juice for lunch.
4. Raymond ate the most.
5. Yes, they had a good time.

PAGE 19   **ANSWERS TO THE WORKBOOK QUESTIONS**   **EXERCISE 2:**
1. London has more beautiful buildings than Calcutta.
2. Switzerland has higher mountains than France.
3. Horses run faster than dogs.
4. Canada is larger than Italy.
5. Spanish hockey players are the worst.
6. Antarctica is colder than South America.
7. Melbourne has fewer people than London.
8. Southern India is hotter than Canada.

PAGE 20   **ANSWERS TO THE WORKBOOK QUESTIONS**   **EXERCISE 3:**
1. This is the best time of year.
2. January is the best time of year. January is the worst…. January is the coldest…
3. Winter is colder in Northern Canada than in _____.
4. I don't like _____ as well as _____.
5. Russia is the biggest country in the world.

PAGE 20   **ANSWERS TO THE WORKBOOK QUESTIONS**   **EXERCISE 4:**

Brian and Pam's **_cousins_** Raymond and Ruth, are visiting them in Canada. They are **_from_** Melbourne, Australia. They are having a good time visiting the lakes and the department stores. Ruth is interested **_in_** new clothes, but Pam is **_more_** interested in sports. Pam thinks the sports equipment, shoes and sports clothes are **_the most_** interesting. Ruth wants to look at all the clothes. Brian is **_interested in_** the soccer equipment but Raymond likes the many kinds of sports clothes **_the best_**.

PAGE 20   ANSWERS TO THE WORKBOOKBOOK QUESTIONS
EXERCISE 5:

1. **Do people drink tea beside the rivers in your town?**
   Yes, people drink tea beside the rivers in my town. No, people don't drink tea beside the rivers in my town.
2. **Do you like cheese and pickle sandwiches?**
   Yes, I like cheese and pickle sandwiches.
   No, I don't like cheese and pickle sandwiches.
3. **Do you like a restaurant better than a picnic?**
   Yes, I like a restaurant better than a picnic.
   No, I don't like a restaurant better than a picnic.
4. **Do people in your country eat sandwiches?**
   Yes, people in my country eat sandwiches.
   No, people in my country don't eat sandwiches.

teacher Guide

Lesson 10
ORAL QUESTIONS

Are you wearing a T-shirt today?

Is _____ wearing a T-shirt today?

Is _____ wearing a baseball hat today?

Does _____ have brown eyes?

Are you wearing a black jacket?

Does _____ have long hair?

Is this a beautiful small town?

Yes, I'm wearing a T-shirt today.
No, I'm not wearing a T-shirt today. Yes, _____ is wearing a T-shirt today. No, _____ isn't wearing a T-shirt today. Yes, _____ is wearing a baseball hat. No, _____ isn't wearing a baseball hat. Yes, _____ has brown eyes.
No, _____ doesn't have brown eyes. Yes, I'm wearing a black jacket.
No, I'm not wearing a black jacket. Yes, _____ has long hair.
No, _____ doesn't have long hair. Yes, this is a beautiful small town.

PAGE 21　　　ANSWERS TO THE WORKBOOK QUESTIONS　　　EXERCISE 1:
1. He eats big hamburgers for supper.
2. I saw a big black dog last week.
3. Three beautiful girls went to the theater.
4. I saw a big black car in town yesterday.
5. He had a red cotton T-shirt.

PAGE 21　　　ANSWERS TO THE WORKBOOK QUESTIONS　　　EXERCISE 2:
1. I wore a _____ _____ _____ to town.
2. I saw a _____ _____ _____ car today.
3. My friend wore a _____ _____ _____ today.
4. I saw a _____ _____ _____ bird today.

PAGE 22　　　ANSWERS TO THE WORKBOOK QUESTIONS　　　EXERCISE 3:
1. Yes, there are many _____ birds in the _____ parks here.
2. Yes, there are many _____ people in Paris.
3. Yes, there are many _____ students here. / No, there aren't many ___ students here.
4. Yes, there is some _____ coffee on the table. / No, there isn't any _____ coffee on the table.
5. Yes, there are _____ soccer players in my country.

PAGE 23　　　ANSWERS TO THE WORKBOOK QUESTIONS　　　EXERCISE 4:
1. What am I going to find?
2. Who am I going to see?
3. When am I going to know?
4. What am I going to need?
5. Where am I going to live?
6. Who am I going to tell?
7. When am I going to return?
8. Where am I going to go?

PAGE 23　　　ANSWERS TO THE WORKBOOK QUESTIONS　　　ACTIVITY 4:
1. ____ has a pen in his/her hand.
   ____ doesn't have a pen in his/her hand.
2. ____ got time-off from work last week. ____ didn't get time-off from work last week.
3. ____ loves to buy new clothes.
   ____ doesn't love to buy new clothes.
4. ____ likes ___ the best.
5. ____ is going to go to the park today.
   ____ isn't going to go to the park today.
6. ____ has brown hair.
   ____ doesn't have brown hair.

Teacher Guide

Lesson 11

ORAL QUESTIONS

Did you eat your breakfast hungrily today?	Yes, I ate my breakfast hungrily today. No, I didn't eat my breakfast hungrily today. Yes, the buses leave town hourly.
Do the buses leave town hourly?	No, the buses don't leave town hourly. Yes, the trains move slowly.
Do the trains move slowly?	No, the trains don't move slowly.
Do you watch TV nightly?	Yes, I watch TV nightly. No, I don't watch TV nightly.
Was your work done quickly today?	Yes, my work was done quickly today. No, my work wasn't done quickly today. Yes, I drive carefully.
Do you drive carefully?	
Do you go to a big city monthly?	Yes, I go to a big city monthly. No, I don't go to a big city monthly.
Do you play basketball well?	Yes, I play basketball well. No, I don't play basketball well.
Do you eat quickly?	Yes, I eat quickly. No, I don't eat quickly.
Are you inside?	Yes, I'm inside
Do you walk slowly?	Yes, I walk slowly. No, I don't walk slowly.
Do your friends talk politely?	Yes, my friends talk politely. No, my friends don't talk politely.
Were you running fast today?	Yes, I was running fast today. No, I wasn't running fast today.
Is there some sunshine today?	Yes, there is some sunshine today. No, there isn't any sunshine today.

PAGE 24 **ANSWERS TO THE WORKBOOK QUESTIONS** **EXERCISE 1:**

1. I cross the street carefully / quickly / slowly.
2. I talk to old people politely / nicely.
3. I work carefully / slowly / quickly.
4. A plane travels quickly.
5. An old man walks slowly.
6. I eat supper hungrily / quickly / politely.

Teacher Guide

Lesson 11 Continued

PAGE 24 **ANSWERS TO THE WORKBOOK QUESTIONS** **EXERCISE 2:**

1. They were <u>busy</u> with their work.
2. The man was extremely <u>heavy</u>.
3. The buses left every <u>hour</u>.
4. Her words were very <u>sad</u>.
5. He did <u>nice</u> work.
6. The girl was <u>glad</u> to get the job.
7. Each piece of bread was <u>thin</u>.
8. He washes every <u>night</u>.

They worked *busily*. He moved *heavily*. The buses left *hourly*. She talked *sadly*. He worked *nicely*. She took it *gladly*. The bread was cut *thinly*. He washes *nightly*.

PAGE 24 **ANSWERS TO THE WORKBOOK QUESTIONS** **ACTIVITY 1:**

1. I play basketball well. / I don't play basketball well.
2. I sing well. / I don't sing well.
3. I ride a bicycle well. / I don't ride a bicycle well.
4. I sleep (very) well. / I don't sleep (very) well.

PAGE 25 **ANSWERS TO THE WORKBOOK QUESTIONS** **EXERCISE 3:**

1. They cut the bread <u>very</u> thinly.
2. She had her hair cut <u>very / extremely</u> short.
3. They hadn't eaten since breakfast so they ate <u>hungrily / quickly</u>.
4. The girl was <u>very</u> tired so she walked <u>slowly</u>.
5. He didn't have a good day because things were going <u>badly / very badly</u>.
6. He was kind to her so she helped him <u>gladly</u>.
7. Her friend was <u>very / extremely</u> sad, so she walked home <u>sadly / slowly</u>.
8. The children looked beautiful, they ran <u>well / beautifully</u>.

PAGE 26 **ANSWERS TO THE WORKBOOK QUESTIONS** **ACTIVITY 3:**
BINGO
Note: Some students may decide to play using the numbers.
That won't help them to learn the vocabulary. Do <u>not</u> call the numbers when playing.

1	fast	slow	13	heavy	light
2	tall	short	14	mother	father
3	blue eyes	brown eyes	15	outside	inside
4	aunt	uncle	16	cold	hot
5	the best	the worst	17	sun	rain
6	young	old	18	black	white
7	walk	run	19	night	day
8	the most	the least	20	well dressed	badly dressed
9	brother	sister	21	love	hate
10	happy	sad	22	small	big
11	smart	stupid	23	morning	evening
12	good	bad	24	last	first

Teacher Guide

Lesson 12 Review

PAGE 27 ANSWERS TO THE WORKBOOK QUESTIONS **EXERCISE 1:**

1. How do you think he sing? (joyfully, beautifully, sadly) *He sings _____.*
2. How is he dressed? (formally, informally) *He is dressed formally.*
3. How do you think he sings? (loudly, softly) *He sings _____.*
4. How do you think she moves? (beautifully, joyfully, quickly) *She moves _____.*
5. How do they dress? (formally, informally) *They dress formally.*
6. How do you think they dance? (slowly, beautifully) *They dance _____.*
7. How do you think the girls dance? (happily, joyfully) *The girls dance _____.*
8. How are they dressed? (formally, informally) *They are dressed informally.*
9. How does the turtle run? (quickly, slowly, beautifully) *It runs _____.*
10. How does he work? (carefully, sadly, happily) *He works carefully.*

PAGE 28 ANSWERS TO THE WORKBOOK QUESTIONS **EXERCISE 2:**

1. have, jacket, Do, a, red, you, ? *Do you have a red jacket?*
2. black, has, long, She, hair *She has long black hair.*
3. small, She, hat, a, has *She has a small hat.*
4. T-shirt, colorful, wore, He, a *He wore a colorful T-shirt.*
5. blue, They, shirts, wanted, cotton *They wanted blue cotton shirts.*

PAGE 28 ANSWERS TO THE WORKBOOK QUESTIONS **EXERCISE 3:**

1. Which picture has the fewest people?
   Picture 1 has the fewest people.

2. Which picture has the most students pulling in the tug-of-war? *Picture 2 has the most students pulling. (in the tug-of war)*

NOTE: It would be correct to answer this question without repeating "in the tug-of-war" because the reference is clear. If there were other pictures of things being pulled it would be necessary to include "in the tug-of-war".

3. In which picture are they the closest to the trees? *They are the closest to the trees in Picture 2.*

4. Which picture has the strongest guy pulling?
   Picture 1 has the strongest guy pulling.

Teacher Guide

Lesson 12 Continued

> **ACTIVITY 3:** This is best done with the whole class.
> Have the students sit in two rows (teams) facing each other.
> Give each student some questions to ask members of the other row (team).
> **NOTE:** The verb at the end of some of these questions and answers is grammatically correct but it often isn't used in spoken language.

Did you get to class earlier than _____
Yes, I got to class earlier than _____.
No, I didn't get to class earlier than _____.

Did you get to class later than _____? Yes, I got to class later than _____.
No, I didn't get to class later than _____.

Which car is the cheapest?
A _____ is the cheapest.

Which car is the most expensive?
A _____ is the most expensive.

Are you taller than your friend (is)? Yes, I'm taller than my friend (is).
No, I'm not taller than my friend (is).

Are you shorter than your father (is)? Yes, I'm shorter than my father (is).
No, I'm not shorter than my father (is).

Are you as tall as your mother (is)?
Yes, I'm as tall as my mother (is).
No, I'm not as tall as my mother (is).

Are you older than your friend (is)?
Yes, I'm older than my friend (is).
No, I'm not older than my friend (is).

Is November the worst month of the year?
Yes, November is the worst month.
No, November isn't the worst month.

Is July better than March?
Yes, July is better than March.
No, July isn't better than March.

Are children hungrier than adults (are)?
Yes, children are hungrier than adults (are).
No, children aren't hungrier than adults (are).

Is July the hottest time of year?
Yes, July is the hottest time of year.
No, July isn't the hottest time of year.

Which month is the worst?
_____ is the worst.

Is a train heavier than a car?
Yes, a train is heavier than a car.

Are some roads narrower than others (are)?
Yes, some roads are narrower than others (are).

Is a bicycle faster than a plane?
No, a bicycle isn't faster than a plane.

Teacher Guide

TEST 3   Lessons 9 to 12

NAME: _____

Answer the questions in sentences. (4 marks each)

1. _____
2. _____
3. _____
4. _____
5. _____

Answer these questions in sentences using one of the suggested comparisons. (4 marks each)

6. What country don't you like? (as well as)

   _____

7. Is American food good? (the best, the worst, not as good as)

   _____

8. Is this a good time of year? (the best, not as good as, the worst)

   _____

Put these words into the right word order. (4 marks each)

9. red, has, He, two, pens, new

   _____

10. long, wore, The, blue, girls, dresses

    _____

Choose the best adverb to complete the sentences. (2 marks each)

hourly   quickly   very   slowly   well

11. His hair was cut _____ short.

12. They were very hungry. They ate _____.

13. The lovers were walking _____.

14. The buses left every hour. They left _____.

15. He did good work. He worked _____.

Teacher Guide   34

Lesson 12 Continued

ORAL QUESTIONS FOR TEST 3

1. Is your friend taller than you are?
2. Are you wearing a red T-shirt today?
3. Do you live in a beautiful small town?
4. Do buses move slowly?
5. Do you play basketball well?

ANSWERS TO THE ORAL QUESTIONS FOR TEST 3

1. *Yes, my friend is taller than I am. (me)*
   No, my friend isn't taller than I am. (me)
2. *Yes, I'm wearing a red T-shirt today. No, I'm not wearing a red T-shirt today.*
3. *Yes, I live in a beautiful small town. No, I don't live in a beautiful small town.*
4. *Yes, buses move slowly.*
   No, buses don't move slowly.
   No, buses move quickly.
5. *Yes, I play basketball well.*
   No, I don't play basketball well.

Answer these questions in sentences using one of the suggested comparisons.

6. What country don't you like? (as well as)
   I don't like _____ as well as _____.
7. Is American food good? (the best, the worst, not as good as)
   American food is _____. / not as good as _____.
8. Is this a good time of year? (the best, not as good as ____, the worst)
   Yes, it's the best time of year.
   No, it's not as good a time of year as _____.
   No, it's the worst time of year.

Put these words into the right word order.

9. red, has, He, two, pens, new
   He has two new red pens.
10. long, wore, The, blue, girls, dresses
    The girls wore long blue dresses.

Choose the best adverb to complete the sentences.

hourly   quickly   very   slowly   well

11. His hair was cut *very* short.
12. They were very hungry. They ate *quickly* / *well*.
13. The lovers were walking *slowly / quickly* / *well*.
14. The buses left every hour. They left *hourly*.
15. He did good work. He worked *well*.

Lesson 13

ORAL QUESTIONS

Do you often buy clothes?	Yes, I often buy clothes. No, I don't often buy clothes.
Do you sometimes take the bus?	Yes, I sometimes take the bus. No, I never take the bus.
Do you always wear shoes?	Yes, I always wear shoes. No, I don't always wear shoes.
Do you usually buy bus tickets?	Yes, I usually buy bus tickets. No, I don't usually buy bus tickets.
Do you frequently ride on a horse?	Yes, I frequently ride on a horse. No, I hardly ever ride on a horse.
Do you often phone your friend?	Yes, I often phone my friend. No, I don't often phone my friend.
Do you frequently travel to Shanghai?	Yes, I frequently travel to Shanghai. No, I hardly ever travel to Shanghai.
Do you usually dress casually?	Yes, I usually dress casually. No, I don't usually dress casually.
Do you sometimes go swimming?	Yes, I sometimes go swimming. No, I hardly ever go swimming.
Do you often go to bed at midnight?	Yes, I often go to bed at midnight. No, I don't often go to bed at midnight.
Do you generally have fruit for lunch?	Yes, I generally have fruit for lunch. No, I don't generally have fruit for lunch.
Do you frequently go out at night?	Yes, I frequently go out at night. No, I never / hardly ever go out at night.
Do you often take the bus to school?	Yes, I often take the bus to school. No, I don't often take the bus to school.
Do you sometimes walk in the park?	Yes, I sometimes walk in the park. No, I never walk in the park.
Do you frequently go to the town?	Yes, I frequently go to the town. No, I never go to town.
Do you often go to Vancouver?	Yes, I often go to Vancouver. No, I never go to Vancouver.
Do you usually eat bananas for breakfast?	Yes, I usually eat bananas for breakfast. No, I don't usually eat bananas for breakfast.
Do you generally ride a horse on the weekends?	Yes, I generally ride a horse on the... No, I don't generally / never ride a horse...
Do you often have juice for breakfast?	Yes, I often have juice for breakfast. No, I never have juice for breakfast.

Teacher Guide

Lesson 13 Continued

PAGE 29   ANSWERS TO THE WORKBOOK QUESTIONS   EXERCISE 1:

1. Jim takes the bus to work. (always) — *Jim always takes the bus to work.*
2. Brent plays soccer on Saturdays. (usually) — *Brent usually plays soccer on Saturdays.*
3. Maria likes to play basketball. (always) — *Maria always likes to play basketball.*
4. John cooks dinner. (often) — *John often cooks dinner.*
5. Sarah dresses casually. (generally) — *Sarah generally dresses casually.*
6. Raymond rides on horses. (never) — *Raymond never rides on horses.*
7. Penny phones her friend. (frequently) — *Penny frequently phones her friend.*
8. Lucy had a party. (just) — *Lucy just had a party.*
9. Ben goes swimming. (hardly ever) — *Ben hardly ever goes swimming.*
10. Mark went walking. (just) — *Mark just went walking.*
11. Lewis wore a T-shirt. (probably) — *Lewis probably wore a T-shirt.*
12. Maria buys a train ticket. (sometimes) — *Maria sometimes buys a train ticket.*
13. Alexander travels to Canada. (often) — *Alexander often travels to Canada.*
14. Bob goes to the movies on Saturdays. (always) — *Bob always goes to the movies on…*
15. Is Mary wearing a mask? — *Yes, she is wearing a mask.*

PAGE 30   ANSWERS TO WORKBOOK QUESTIONS   EXERCISE 2:

1. Do you eat pizza? — *Yes, I often / sometimes eat pizza. No, I never eat pizza.*
2. Do you play basketball? — *Yes, I frequently / often play basketball. No, I never / seldom play basketball.*
3. Do you stay up all night? — *Yes, I sometimes stay up all night. No, I never stay up all night.*
4. Do you go swimming? — *Yes, I frequently / often / sometimes go swimming. No, I never go swimming.*
5. Do you get hungry at noon? — *Yes, I always / usually get hungry at noon. No, I don't usually get hungry at noon.*
6. Do you meet your friends at the lake? — *Yes, I often meet my friends at the lake. No, I seldom / never meet my friends at the lake.*
7. Do you eat Chinese food? — *Yes, I often eat Chinese food. No, I never eat Chinese food.*
8. Do you eat breakfast in a restaurant? — *Yes, I usually eat breakfast in a restaurant. No, I hardly ever eat breakfast in a restaurant.*
9. Do you buy expensive clothes? — *Yes, I frequently buy expensive clothes. No, I hardly ever buy expensive clothes.*
10. Do you pick up your friends in a car? — *Yes, I occasionally pick up my friends in a car. No, I never pick up my friends in a car.*
11. Do you sleep at home? — *Yes, I always / usually sleep at home. No, I don't usually / never sleep at home.*
12. Do you enjoy eating vegetables? — *Yes, I usually / often enjoy eating vegetables. No, I never enjoy eating vegetables.*

Teacher Guide

Lesson 13 Continued

PAGE 24 **ANSWERS TO STUDENT READER QUESTIONS** **ACTIVITY 2:**
Suggested answers:

1. Tom was very tired of working.

2. *No, they hardly ever go to concerts.*

3. *No, they seldom go out.*

4. *Yes, their theaters usually have good concerts.*

5. *Yes, Peter and Sarah often go to concerts. Yes, Sarah and Peter go to many concerts.*

PAGE 30 **ANSWERS TO THE WORKBOOK QUESTIONS** **EXERCISE 3:**

to dress	to put clothes on
to stay up	to go to bed late
frequently	often
hardly ever	seldom
occasionally	sometimes likely
probably	you eat them to
vegetables	leave
to go out	not the same
different	

PAGE 31 **ANSWERS TO THE BINGO** **ACTIVITY 4:**

2	frequently	8	seldom	14	likely	24	generally
20	sometimes	3	finally	9	badly	15	slowly
21	hourly	4	monthly	10	thinly	16	quickly
22	sadly	5	nightly	11	extremely polite	23	a piece
6	to agree	12	the least	17	to sing well	18	close to
19	expensive	13	to start	7	time off	1.	to leave

Teacher Guide

Lesson 14

Note to the teacher: "to sleep in" means to stay in bed longer than usual in the morning. "never" can be used instead of "don't ever"

ORAL QUESTIONS

Do you ever dress formally?	*Yes, I dress formally.* *No, I never dress formally.*
Do you ever have fruit for breakfast?	*Yes, I sometimes have fruit for breakfast.* *No, I don't ever have fruit for breakfast.*
Do you ever buy coffee?	*Yes, I buy coffee.* *No, I don't ever / never buy coffee.*
Do you ever see your friends?	*Yes, I frequently see my friends.* *No, I don't ever / never see my friends. Yes,*
Do you ever sleep in?	*I often sleep in.* *No, I don't ever / never sleep in.*
Do you ever go to Rome?	*Yes, I go to Rome.* *No, I don't ever / never go to Rome.*
Do you ever see your mother?	*Yes, I see my mother.* *No, I don't ever see my mother.*
Do you ever travel to the United States?	*Yes, I travel to the United States.* *No, I don't ever travel to the United States.* *No, I never travel to the United States. Yes,*
Do you ever play basketball?	*I play basketball.* *No, I don't ever play basketball.*

FORMING QUESTIONS - ORAL QUESTIONS:
Give the students these sentences: (They are to make the question using "ever".)

They played basketball.	*Did they ever play basketball? Did*
He walked to work.	*he ever walk to work?*
She went to the church.	*Did she ever go to the church? Did*
They drove to town.	*they ever drive to town? Did he*
He saw his friend in town.	*ever see his friend in town? Did it*
It rained all night.	*ever rain all night?*
He walked slowly.	*Did he ever walk slowly?*

PAGE 32 ANSWERS TO THE WORKBOOK QUESTIONS **EXERCISE 1:**

1. *Did you ever see a ghost?*
2. *Do you ever buy theatre tickets?*
3. *Did you ever watch TV?*
4. *Do you ever walk with your dog?*
5. *Did you ever walk in the forest?*
6. *Did you ever hike through the snow?*

7. *Did you ever ride a bicycle?*
8. *Did you ever see a dragon?*

Yes, I saw a ghost. / No, I didn't ever see a ghost. Yes, I buy theatre tickets. / No, I don't ever buy… Yes, I / we watched TV. / No, I / we don't ever watch… Yes, I walk with my dog. / No, I don't ever walk… Yes, I walked in the forest. No, I didn't ever walk… Yes, I hiked through the snow.
No, I didn't ever hike through the snow.
Yes, I rode a bicycle ./ No, I didn't ever ride a bicycle.
Yes, I saw a dragon. No, I didn't ever see a dragon.

Teacher Guide

Lesson 14 Continued

NOTE: "Never" could be used in any of the Exercise 1 answers.

1. Did you ever see a ghost?
2. Do you ever buy theatre tickets?
3. Did you ever watch TV?
4. Do you ever walk with your dog?
5. Did you ever walk in the forest?
6. Did you ever hike through the snow?
7. Did you ever ride a bicycle?
8. Did you ever see a dragon?

Yes, I saw a ghost. / No, I never saw a ghost. Yes, I buy theatre tickets. / No, I never buy… Yes, I watched TV. / No, I never watched TV. Yes, I walk with my dog. / No, I never walk… Yes, I walked in the forest. No, I never walked… Yes, I hiked through the snow. No, I never … Yes, I rode a bicycle ./ No, I never rode a bicycle. Yes, I saw a dragon. No, I never saw a dragon.

PAGE 26   ANSWERS TO THE STUDENT READER QUESTIONS   ACTIVITY 2:

1. **Do you ever go to the <u>theater</u>?**
   Yes, he / she goes to the theater.
   No, he / she doesn't ever go to the theater.
   No, he / she never goes to the theater.

2. **Do you ever eat *bananas*.**
   Yes, he / she eats bananas.
   No, he / she doesn't ever eat bananas. No, he / she never eats bananas.

3. **Do you ever go *<u>swimming</u>*?**
   Yes, he / she goes swimming.
   No, he / she doesn't ever go swimming. No, he / she never goes swimming.

4. **Do you ever take *<u>the / a bus</u>*?**
   Yes, he / she takes the bus.
   No, he / she never takes the bus.

5. **Do you ever read *<u>a book</u>*?**
   Yes, he / she read a book.
   No, he / she didn't ever read a book. No, he / she never read a book.

6. **Do you ever see *<u>your friends</u>*?**
   Yes, he / she sees his / her friends. No, he / she doesn't ever see his / her…No, he / she never sees his / her friends.

7. **Do you ever go <u>hiking</u>?**
   Yes, he / she goes hiking.
   No, he / she doesn't go hiking.
   No, he / she never goes hiking.

8. **Do you ever drive *<u>a car</u>*?**
   Yes, he / she drives a car.
   No, he / she doesn't ever drive a car. No, he / she never drives a car.

9. **Do you ever wear a dress?**
   Yes, he / she wears a dress.
   No, he / she never wears a dress.

Teacher Guide

Lesson 15

ORAL QUESTIONS

USING ADVERBS WITH THE VERB "TO BE"

Are you usually hungry?	*Yes, I'm usually hungry.*
	No, I'm not usually hungry.
Are you often cold?	*Yes, I'm often cold.*
	No, I'm not often cold.
Is she often casually dressed?	*Yes, she is often casually dressed.*
	No, she isn't often casually dressed.
Is he often wearing a watch?	*Yes, he's often wearing a watch.*
	No, he isn't often wearing a watch.
Is it always dark at night?	*Yes, it's always dark at night.*
Is the bus always crowded?	*Yes, the bus is always crowded.*
	No, the bus isn't always crowded.
Is it ever cold in January?	*Yes, it's sometimes / always cold in January. No, it isn't ever cold in January.*
Are you often tired?	*Yes, I'm often tired.*
	No, I'm not often tired.
Are there many tourists in your city?	*Yes, there are many tourists in my (our) city. No, there aren't many tourists in my (our) city. Yes, I go to town.*
Do you ever go to town?	
Did you ever want something to eat?	*Yes, I wanted something to eat.*
Will you probably see your friend tomorrow?	*Yes, I'll likely / probably see my friend tomorrow.*
	No, I won't likely see my friend tomorrow.

PAGE 34	ANSWERS TO THE WORKBOOK QUESTIONS	EXERCISE 1:

1. *Victoria is a beautiful city.*
2. *Some very unfortunate people live there.*
3. *Lonely people often drink alcohol.*
4. *Unfortunate people often need help.*
5. *Alcohol doesn't usually help people.*
6. *There are many unfortunate people in most cities.*
7. *Handicapped people often have many problems.*
8. *They can't find a job*

PAGE 34	ANSWERS TO THE WORKBOOK QUESTIONS	EXERCISE 2:

world	all the countries and waters
street people	they live on the streets
handicapped	people who can't see, walk or talk well people
people drugs	take them to change the way they think not
dark	much light
rich people alcohol	they have a lot of money
problem	people drink it
	what happens isn't good

Lesson 15 Continued

PAGE 35   ANSWERS TO THE WORKBOOK QUESTIONS   EXERCISE 3:

1. Are there many street people in your town?
   Yes, there are many street people in my town.
   No, there aren't many street people in my town.
2. Do street people have bad times?
   Yes, they have (very) bad times.
3. What problem might a handicapped person have?
   They might have a problem seeing / walking / or / talking.

4. Do many people who aren't handicapped drink alcohol?
   Yes, many people (who aren't handicapped) drink alcohol.
5. Do you think that alcohol helps people?
   I think that alcohol doesn't usually help people.
   I think that alcohol sometimes helps people.
6. How do the street people often feel?
   They often feel alone.

7. What will make someone's problems worse?
   Drugs will make someone's problems worse.
8. What do the street people need?
   They need help / food / love / friends.
9. Do beautiful gardens help the street people?
   No, beautiful gardens don't usually help the street people.

10. We say, "The world walks by". What does that mean?
    It means that the people walk past the street people without thinking about them.
11. Where do most of the street people live?
    Most of the street people live on the streets.

12. Have you ever faced a bad problem?
    Yes, I've faced a bad problem. No, I haven't.

PAGE 28   ANSWERS TO THE STUDENT READER QUESTIONS   ACTIVITY 3:

1. Isn't it?   2. Isn't he?   3. Isn't it?   4. Are there?   5. Won't he?

Teacher Guide

Lesson 15 Continued

ACTIVITY 5: This is best done with the whole class.
Have the students sit in two rows (team) facing each other.
Give each student some questions to ask members of the other row (team).
All students should ask and answer some questions.

Do you sometimes walk in the forest?
Yes, I sometimes walk in the forest.
No, I never (don't ever) walk in the forest.

Do you ever wear a hat?
Yes, I (usually, often, sometimes) wear a hat. No, I never (don't ever) wear a hat.

Do you sometimes go swimming?
Yes, I sometimes (often) go swimming.
No, I never (don't ever) go swimming.

Do you frequently take a bus?
Yes, I frequently take a bus.
No, I never (don't ever) take a bus.

Do you usually ride a bicycle to class?
Yes, I usually ride a bicycle to class.
No, I never ride a bicycle to class.

Are you going to play basketball tonight? *Yes, I'm going to play basketball tonight.*
No, I'm not going to play basketball…

Do you ever go to Bombay?
Yes, I go to Bombay.
No, I never (don't ever) go to Bombay.

Do you sometimes go to work on Saturdays?
Yes, I sometimes go to work on Saturdays.
No, I never (don't ever) go to work on Saturdays.

Do you ever take the train?
Yes, I take the train.
No, I never (don't ever) take the train.

Do you often eat supper at 10:00 p.m.?
Yes, I sometimes eat supper at 10:00 p.m..
No, I never eat supper at 10:00 p.m..

Are you often in the stores?
Yes, I'm often (sometimes) in the stores.
No, I'm never (hardly ever) in the stores.

Do you ever go to the movies on Saturdays?
Yes, I go to the movies on Saturdays.
No, I never go to the movies on Saturdays.

Do you ever have pizza for supper?
Yes, I have pizza for supper.
No, I never (seldom) have pizza for supper.

Do you ever come to class on foot?
Yes, I come to class on foot.
No, I never (don't ever) come to class on foot.

Do you usually drink coffee on the weekend?
Yes, I usually drink coffee on the weekend.
No, I never drink coffee on the weekend.

Do you always watch TV at night?
Yes, I always (usually) watch TV at night.
No, I never (don't ever) watch TV at night.

Lesson 16

ORAL QUESTIONS

Do you often walk to town? Are
you usually at home at night? Are
you frequently at the stores?

Are you often in the park with your friend?

Do you welcome your friends to your home?
Do you usually have vegetables for dinner?

Do you often sleep in?

Is it always dark at night?

Do visitors usually come to your town?

Is your town very crowded?

Do you frequently buy tea?

Do you always feel welcome in this class?
Did you <u>sleep in</u> this morning?

Are the mountains a lonely place?
(sometimes, never)
Are you <u>interested in</u> music?

Yes, I often walk to town.
No, I seldom / never walk to town.
Yes, I'm usually at home at night.
No, I'm not usually at home at night.
Yes, I'm frequently at the stores.
No, I'm not frequently at the stores.
Yes, I'm often in the park with my friend.
No, I'm not often in the park with my friend. No, I don't have a friend.

Yes, I welcome my friends to my home.
Yes, I usually have vegetables for dinner.
No, I don't usually have vegetables for dinner. Yes, I often sleep in.
No, I don't often sleep in.
Yes, it's always dark at night.

Yes, visitors usually come to our / my town.
No, visitors seldom / never come to my / our town.
　　Yes, my / our town is very crowded.
No, my / our town isn't very crowded.
Yes, I frequently buy tea.
No, I don't usually buy tea.

Yes, I always feel welcome here. / in this class. Yes, I slept in this morning.
No, I didn't sleep in this morning.
Yes, the mountains are sometimes a lonely place.
No, the mountains are never a lonely place. Yes, I'm interested in music.
No, I'm not interested in music.

PAGE 36　　　**ANSWERS TO THE WORKBOOK QUESTIONS**　　**EXERCISE 1:**

1. What do you think the name "The Open Door" means? *It means that everyone is welcome.*
2. Who goes there?
   The street people go there. The volunteers go there.
3. Who gives bread to The Open Door?
   The stores give bread to The Open Door.
4. Do volunteer workers do a lot of the work there? *Yes, they do. / Yes, they do a lot of work there.*
5. Do you have a place like The Open Door in your city?
   Yes, we do. / Yes, we have a place like The Open Door.
   No, we don't have a place like The Open Door.
6. What do you think is the best about The Open Door? *I think …*

Teacher Guide

Lesson 16 Continued

PAGE 30 **POSSIBLE ANSWERS - STUDENT READER QUESTIONS ACTIVITY 2:**
1. *They could: be friendly / give food / remember some birthdays*
2. *It gives them something to do. / It makes them feel needed.*
3. *It's a comfortable place to be. / They can use a telephone. / They can get their mail there.*

PAGE 36 **ANSWERS TO THE WORKBOOK QUESTIONS** **EXERCISE 2:**

living room	*a comfortable place*
newspaper	*you read it*
to	*to work for no money*
volunteer	*perhaps*
maybe	*to take something to a place*
to bring	*to stay in bed in the morning*
to sleep in	

PAGE 36 **ANSWERS TO THE WORKBOOK QUESTIONS** **EXERCISE 3:**

In Victoria there is a place called The Open Door. It gives the <u>street people</u> a warm and <u>comfortable</u> place to go. When they are there, they can get a free cup of <u>tea</u> or coffee and something to eat. They can also read a <u>newspaper</u> and talk to their friends.
The people who do <u>volunteer</u> work there don't want to be given any <u>money</u>. They feel <u>good</u> when they go home because they have helped someone <u>else</u>.

PAGE 37 **SUGGESTED ANSWERS TO THE WORKBOOK QUESTIONS ACTIVITY 5:**

Bill: Hi Joe! How are you doing?
Joe: *I'm okay. / I'm not so good.*
Bill: What are you doing this morning?
Joe: *I don't know. / What can I do?/ I'm not doing anything.*
Bill: Let's walk to The Open Door.
We can get a cup of coffee, it's cold today.
Joe: *Okay. / Sure. / Good idea. / Yes, it's nice and warm in there.*
Bill: I want to talk to someone. Maybe they can help me.
Joe: *Another problem? / They are helpful there.*
Bill: My mother is sick and I have no money to get home.
Joe: *I don't know. / Maybe they can help. / Let's go.*

PAGE 37 **ANSWERS TO THE WORKBOOK QUESTIONS** **EXERCISE 4:**

1. The street people are always hungry, <u>aren't they</u>?   <u>Yes, they are.</u>
2. The Open Door is a warm place, <u>isn't it</u>?   <u>Yes, it is.</u>
3. Bill's mother is sick, <u>isn't she</u>?   <u>Yes, she is.</u>
4. Bill wants to go home, <u>doesn't he</u>?   <u>Yes, he does.</u>
5. Someone can help Bill, <u>can't they</u>?   <u>Yes, they can.</u>
6. There are street people in your city, <u>aren't there</u>?   <u>Yes, there are.</u>
7. Volunteer work makes you feel good, <u>doesn't it</u>?   <u>Yes, it does.</u>
8. Victoria has beautiful gardens, <u>hasn't it</u> / <u>doesn't it</u>?   <u>Yes, it has.</u> / <u>Yes, it does.</u>

teacher Guide

Lesson 16 Continued

ORAL QUESTIONS FOR TEST 4
1. Did you ever go hiking?

2. Is it always dark at night?
3. Do you often drink juice for breakfast?

4. Do you usually sleep in?

5. Will you likely have a holiday this year?

ANSWERS
Yes, I went hiking.
No, I didn't ever go hiking.
Yes, it's always dark at night.
Yes, I often drink juice for breakfast. No, I don't ever (never) drink juice for… Yes, I usually sleep in.
No, I don't usually sleep in.
Yes, I'll likely have a holiday this year. No, I won't likely have a holiday this year.

ANSWERS TO THE WRITTEN SECTION OF TEST 4
Answer in sentences using one of the adverbs in (brackets).

6. Do some street people go to The Open Door? (usually / never)

7. Do some volunteers work there? (often)
8. Are the street people lonely? (usually/ sometimes)
9. Are there many people at The Open Door? (likely)

10. Do you study your English? (usually, never)

Yes, some street people usually go to The Open Door.
No, some street people never go there.

Yes, some volunteers often work there.
Yes, they are sometimes lonely.
Yes, they are usually lonely.
Yes, there are likely many people there. / at The Open Door.

Yes, I usually study my English.
No, I never study my English.

Put the words into sentence order.

11. are, They, late, very
12. go, They, to, store, often, the

They are very late. They often go to the store.

13. The people want to go somewhere *with* their friends.
14. They are interested *in* visiting different cities.

Lessons 13 to 16   TEST 4

NAME_____   (Questions 1 to 12, 4 marks each)

1. _____
2. _____
3. _____
4. _____
5. _____

Answer in sentences using one of the adverbs in (brackets).

6. Do some people go to The Open Door? (usually / never)

_____

7. Do some volunteers work there? (often)

_____

8. Are the street people lonely? (usually / sometimes)

_____

9. Are there many people at The Open Door? (likely)

_____

10. Do you study your English? (usually, never)

_____

Put the words into sentence order.

11. are, They, late, very

_____

12. go, They, to, store, often, the

_____

Complete these sentences using the best words from below. (1 mark each)

in   with   to   a

The people want to go somewhere 13._____ their friends.

They are interested 14._____ visiting different cities.

Teacher Guide   47

Lesson 17

ORAL QUESTIONS

**The students are to answer using the contractions with would.
The teacher will need to indicate the groups or individuals that the pronouns refer to.**

Would you like some coffee?

Would he / she like some coffee?

Yes, I'd like some coffee.
No, I wouldn't like any coffee.
Yes, he'd / she'd like some coffee.
No, he / she wouldn't like any coffee.

Would you like some pizza?

Would she like some pizza?

Yes, I'd like some pizza.
No, I wouldn't like any pizza.
Yes, she'd like some pizza.
No, she wouldn't like any pizza.

Would you want to go to Canada?

Would they want to go to Canada?

Yes, I'd want to go to Canada.
No, I wouldn't want to go to Canada.
Yes, they'd want to go to Canada.
No, they wouldn't want to go to Canada.

Would you like some mango juice?

Would he / she like some mango juice?

Yes, I'd like some mango juice.
No, I wouldn't like any mango juice.
Yes, he'd / she'd like some mango juice.
No, he / she wouldn't like any mango juice.

Would you like some chocolate? (plural) Would they like some chocolate?

Yes, we'd like some chocolate.
No, we wouldn't like any chocolate.
Yes, they'd like some chocolate.
No, they wouldn't like any chocolate.

Would you order for a friend in a restaurant?

Would he / she order for a friend in a restaurant?

Yes, I'd order for a friend in a restaurant.
No, I wouldn't order for a friend in a restaurant.
Yes, he'd / she'd order for a friend in a…
No, he / she wouldn't order for a friend in a…

Would you like to play soccer this afternoon?

Would he / she like to play soccer this afternoon?

Yes, I'd like to play soccer this afternoon
No, I wouldn't like to play soccer this afternoon.
Yes, he'd / she'd like to play soccer this…
No, he / she wouldn't like to play soccer …

Would you like some ice cream?

Would he / she like some ice cream?

Yes, I'd like some ice cream.
No, I wouldn't like any ice cream.
Yes, he'd / she'd like some ice cream.
No, he / she wouldn't like any ice cream.

Teacher Guide

Lesson 17 Continued

PAGE 38   **ANSWERS TO THE WORKBOOK QUESTIONS**   **EXERCISE 1:**

1. Would you want to work all night?
   Yes, I'd want to work all night.
   No, I wouldn't want to work all night.

2. Would you order a salad with lettuce and tomatoes?
   Yes, I'd order a salad with lettuce and…
   No, I wouldn't order a salad with… Yes, I'd like some tea.

3. Would you like some tea?
   No, I wouldn't like any tea.

4. Would you go out for dinner?
   Yes, I'd go out for dinner.
   No, I wouldn't go out for dinner.

Note to the teacher: "to go out" means to go away from home for a short time.

5. Would your cat eat a bird?
   Yes, my cat would eat a bird.
   No, my cat wouldn't eat a bird.

6. Would you want to have a cat?
   Yes, I'd want to have a cat.
   No, I wouldn't want to have a cat.

7. Would your dog eat lettuce?
   Yes, my dog would eat lettuce.
   No, my dog wouldn't eat lettuce.

8. Would your friends want to play basketball?
   Yes, my friends would want to play… No, my friends wouldn't want to play…

9. Would you enjoy a crowded restaurant?
   Yes, I'd enjoy a crowded restaurant.
   No. I wouldn't enjoy a crowded restaurant.

PAGE 38   **ANSWERS TO THE WORKBOOK QUESTIONS**   **EXERCISE 2:** Carol and her friends want to order something *in* a restaurant. Carol's friends can't speak English so Carol orders *for* them. Zula says *she'd* like the soup and salad. Berko says *he'd* like the pizza. Carol decides that *she'd* like the noodles. They agree that *they'd* all like a glass of juice. The waiter said that the restaurant was crowded and *it'd* take a few minutes to make the orange juice. They all agreed that it *wouldn't* matter. It'd be okay.

PAGE 39   **ANSWERS TO THE WORKBOOK QUESTIONS**   **EXERCISE 3:**

prefer	*what you like the best*	crowd	*a lot of people*
tomato	*a round red vegetable*	menu	*a list of what you can order*
beverage	*you drink it*	to wish	*to want something*
patron	*a person who eats in a restaurant*	pineapple	*a kind of fruit*
ice cream	*it's very, very cold*	salad	*it has many cold vegetables it's*
lunchroom	*where you eat lunch*	dessert	*hot or cold and usually sweet*

PAGE 39   **ANSWERS TO THE WORKBOOK QUESTIONS**   **EXERCISE 4:**

noodles	*ice cream*	*pie*
crowd	*tomato*	*tea, coffee or hot chocolate*

ACTIVITY 7:   Photocopy and cut the questions into cards.
Divide the class into Team 1 and Team 2, and have them sit facing each other.
Give each student one or two question cards.
A student on Team 1 is to ask the question on his or her card to a student on Team 2.
Next a student on Team 2 is to ask the question on his or her card to a student on Team 1. One point is given for each correct answer.

Teacher Guide

Lesson 17 Continued

Would you order ice cream or pie? hamburger?
I'd order _____

Would your friend want to have a salad? My friend would want to have a _____.

Would you like coffee or juice?
I'd like _____.

Would your friends want noodles?
Yes, they'd want noodles.

Would you eat pineapple pizza?
Yes, I'd eat pineapple pizza.
No, I wouldn't eat pineapple pizza.

Would your friends ask for soup?
Yes, my friends would ask for soup.
No, my friends wouldn't ask for soup.

Would you like to work in a restaurant? Yes, I'd like to work in a restaurant.
No, I wouldn't like to work in a restaurant.

Would your cat eat salad?
No, my cat wouldn't eat salad.

Would you enjoy a hamburger with cheese?
Yes, I'd enjoy a hamburger with cheese.
No, I wouldn't enjoy a hamburger with cheese.

What beverage do you like the best?
I like _____ the best.

Would you ask for pizza or a
I'd ask for _____.

Would your friend order soup or salad?
My friend would order _____.

Would your dog eat lettuce?
No, my dog wouldn't eat lettuce.

Would you ask for hot chocolate or tea?
I'd ask for _____.

Would you like to be a waiter?
Yes, I'd like to be a waiter.
No, I wouldn't like to be a waiter.

Would your dog drink tea?
Yes, my dog would drink tea.
No, my dog wouldn't drink tea.

Would you drink cold coffee?
Yes, I'd drink cold coffee.
No, I wouldn't drink cold coffee.

Would you eat a dog?
No, I wouldn't eat a dog.

Would you order chicken pasta?
Yes, I'd order chicken pasta.
No, I wouldn't order chicken pasta.

What dessert would you order?
I'd order _____.

Teacher Guide

Lesson 18

ORAL QUESTIONS

Are you interested in sports?	*Yes, I'm interested in sports.*
	No, I'm not interested in sports.
When did you arrive at work today?	*I arrived at _____.*
	I didn't arrive at work today.
	I didn't go to work today.
Did you talk about a movie last night?	*Yes, I talked about a movie last night.*
	No, I didn't talk about a movie last night.
Do you wait for your friend every day?	*Yes, I wait for my friend every day.*
	No I don't wait for my friend every day.
Did you ever compete in a tug-of-war?	*Yes, I competed in a tug-of-war.*
	No, I never competed in a tug-of-war.
Do you usually ask for more coffee?	*Yes, I usually ask for more coffee.*
	No, I don't usually ask for more coffee.
Do you like vegetarian food?	*Yes, I like vegetarian food.*
	No, I don't like vegetarian food.
Do you eat a lot of cheese?	*Yes, I eat a lot of cheese.*
	No, I don't eat a lot of cheese.
Did you ask for some juice?	*Yes, I asked for some juice.*
	No, I didn't ask for any juice.
Will you pick up your friend tonight?	*Yes, I'll pick up my friend tonight.*
	No, I won't pick up my friend tonight.
Do you dream about playing hockey?	*Yes, I dream about playing hockey.*
	No, I don't dream about playing hockey.
Will you get time-off from work next week?	*Yes, I'll get time-off from work next week.*
	No, I won't get time-off from work next week.
What kind of drinks do you like?	*I like cold / hot drinks.*
	I like juices.
Do you often sleep in?	*Yes, I often sleep in.*
	No, I don't often sleep in.
Do you ever stay up all night?	*Yes, I (sometimes) stay up all night.*
	No, I never /don't ever stay up all night.
Will you wait for your friend after class? Did	*Yes, I'll wait for my friend after class.*
	No, I won't wait for my friend after class.
you stay up late last night?	*Yes, I stayed up late last night.*
	No, I didn't stay up late last night.
Did you compete in a soccer game yesterday?	*Yes, I competed in a soccer game yesterday. No, I didn't compete in a soccer game…*
Is there a restaurant across from your house?	*Yes, there's a restaurant across from my house. No, there isn't a restaurant across from my house.*

Teacher Guide

Lesson 18 Continued

PAGE 41   ANSWERS TO THE WORKBOOK QUESTIONS   EXERCISE 1:

   Brian and Raymond are in a restaurant. Raymond is sitting across **_from_** Brian. They are **waiting** **_for_** Ruth and Pam. Brian has a hamburger and he asked **_for_** some coffee. He isn't as interested **_in_** Canadian food as Raymond. He is more interested **_in_** sports. He reads many books **_about_** sports and competes **_in_** many games.

   The girls are late arriving **_at_** the restaurant. They stayed **_up_** late last night to study their English and so Pam slept **_in_** this morning. Then she had to pick **_up_** Ruth in her car. Ruth's hotel is farther **_from_** the restaurant **_than_** Pam's house.

PAGE 41   ANSWERS TO THE WORKBOOK QUESTIONS   EXERCISE 2:

Answer these questions using the underlined phrase in the past tense.

1. Did you **sleep in** this morning?
   Yes, I slept in this morning.
   No, I didn't sleep in this morning.
2. Did you **wait for** your friend today?
   Yes, I waited for my friend today.
   No, I didn't wait for my friend today.
3. Did you **pick up** a friend today?
   Yes, I picked up a friend today.
   No, I didn't pick up a friend today.
4. Did you **ask for** help with your English?
   Yes, I asked for help with my English. No, I didn't ask for help with my English.
5. Did you **stay up** late last night?
   Yes, I stayed up late last night.
   No, I didn't stay up late last night.
6. Did you **talk about** the latest movie?
   Yes, I talked about the latest movie.
   No, I didn't talk about the latest movie.
7. Did you **arrive at** class on time?
   Yes, I arrived at class on time.
   No, I didn't arrive at class on time.
8. Did you **ask** your friend **for** help?
   Yes, I asked my friend for help.
   No, I didn't ask my friend for help.
9. Did you live **across from** a school last year?
   Yes, I lived across from a school last year. No, I didn't live across from a school last year.

REVIEW ACTIVITY 5:   **DIRECTIONS**
   The teacher will give each student <u>one role card</u> and one questionnaire.
   The students will then move about the class asking two students the questions
   and answering those of others <u>in sentences</u>.

NOTE:

   Review: <u>in</u> 2005   <u>in</u> April   <u>on</u> January 10th

Teacher Guide

Lesson 18 Continued

Ask Student 1 these questions.   **Write the answers in sentences**

What is your name? _____

Are you married? _____

What month were you born? _____

What day were you born? _____

What year were you born? _____

What is your favorite hobby? _____

****

Ask Student 2 these questions.   **Write the answers in sentences**

What is your name? _____

Are you married? _____

What month were you born? _____

What day were you born? _____

What year were you born? _____

What is your favorite hobby? _____

ROLE CARDS

NAME: Linda Watts
MARITAL STATUS: single
MONTH OF BIRTH: July
DAY OF BIRTH: 22nd
YEAR OF BIRTH: 2000
HOBBIES: writing

NAME: Margaret Selkirk
MARITAL STATUS: single
MONTH OF BIRTH: April
DAY OF BIRTH: 2nd
YEAR OF BIRTH: 2001
HOBBIES: hiking

NAME: Winston Donovan
MARITAL STATUS: single
MONTH OF BIRTH: October
DAY OF BIRTH: 22nd
YEAR OF BIRTH: 1997

NAME: Sally Ray
MARITAL STATUS: married
MONTH OF BIRTH: October
DAY OF BIRTH: 15th
YEAR OF BIRTH: 1998

teacher Guide

Lesson 18 Continued

NAME: Joseph Woods
MARITAL STATUS: single
MONTH OF BIRTH: Aptil
DAY OF BIRTH: 15th
YEAR OF BIRTH: 1999
HOBBIES: gardening

NAME: Deborah Mills
MARITAL STATUS: married
MONTH OF BIRTH: October
DAY OF BIRTH: 10th
YEAR OF BIRTH: 1997
HOBBIES: basketball

NAME: Lynn Nash
MARITAL STATUS: single
MONTH OF BIRTH: September
DAY OF BIRTH: 16th
YEAR OF BIRTH: 2003
HOBBIES: hiking

NAME: Bruce Robertson
MARITAL STATUS: single
MONTH OF BIRTH: April
DAY OF BIRTH: 22nd
YEAR OF BIRTH: 2001
HOBBIES: mountain climbing

NAME: Alan Dunning
MARITAL STATUS: single
MONTH OF BIRTH: May
DAY OF BIRTH: 19th
YEAR OF BIRTH: 2006
HOBBIES: soccer

NAME: Miranda Bates
MARITAL STATUS: single
MONTH OF BIRTH: July
DAY OF BIRTH: 25th
YEAR OF BIRTH: 2001
HOBBIES: computers

NAME: Samuel Munn
MARITAL STATUS: single
MONTH OF BIRTH: March
DAY OF BIRTH: 10th
YEAR OF BIRTH: 2002
HOBBIES: ice hockey

NAME: Brian Patterson
MARITAL STATUS: single
MONTH OF BIRTH: December
DAY OF BIRTH: 3rd
YEAR OF BIRTH: 1999
HOBBIES: soccer

NAME: Adrian (Adrianne) May
MARITAL STATUS: single
MONTH OF BIRTH: August
DAY OF BIRTH: 4th
YEAR OF BIRTH: 2004
HOBBIES: computers

NAME: Penny Cuthbert
MARITAL STATUS: married
MONTH OF BIRTH: December
DAY OF BIRTH: 18th
YEAR OF BIRTH: 1996
HOBBIES: archery

NAME: Elizabeth Fraser
MARITAL STATUS: single
MONTH OF BIRTH: June
DAY OF BIRTH: 28th
YEAR OF BIRTH: 2004
HOBBIES: painting

NAME: Daniela Black
MARITAL STATUS: single
MONTH OF BIRTH: May
DAY OF BIRTH: 11th
YEAR OF BIRTH: 1998
HOBBIES: hiking

Lesson 19

Note to the teacher: The following "CONTRACTIONS WITH HAVE" at the bottom of Page 36 can be used with "got".

he's got   she's got   it's got

ORAL QUESTIONS

Have you got a ghost in your house? Have you got a pen in your pocket? Have you got an interesting hobby?

Yes, I've got a ghost in my house. No, I haven't got a ghost in my house. Yes, I've got a pen in my pocket.
No, I haven't got a pen in my pocket.
Yes, I've got an interesting hobby. No, I haven't got an interesting hobby.

Have you got a good friend?

Have you got long dark hair? Have you got a jacket?

Yes, I've got a good friend.
No, I haven't got a good friend.
Yes, I've got long dark hair.
No, I haven't got long dark hair. Yes, I've got a jacket.
No, I haven't got a jacket.

Have you got glasses?

Have you got a big black dog? Have you got a middle name?

Yes, I've got glasses.
No, I haven't got glasses.
Yes, I've got a big black dog.
No, I haven't got a big black dog. Yes, I've got a middle name.
No, I haven't got a middle name.

Have you got a notebook?

Have you got a cookie?

Have you got a big car?

Yes, I've got a notebook.
No, I haven't got a notebook.
Yes, I've got a cookie.
No, I haven't got a cookie.
Yes, I've got a big car.
No, I haven't got a big car.

Have you got some good books? Have you got some relatives? Have you got a pen?

Yes, I've got some good books.
No, I haven't got any good books. Yes, I've got some relatives.
No, I haven't got any relatives.
Yes, I've got a pen.
No, I haven't got a pen.

Teacher Guide

Lesson 19 Continued

PAGE 36 ANSWERS TO THE STUDENT READER QUESTIONS **ACTIVITY 1:**

1. He has a newspaper.
2. They have a chance to travel.
3. The man has a newspaper.
4. The restaurant has many patrons.
5. The students have some juice.
6. The buildings have many windows.

7. The boy has some pie.
8. The mountains have a lot of snow.

He has got a newspaper.
They have got a chance to travel. The man has got a newspaper.
The restaurant has got many patrons.
The students have got some juice. The buildings have got many windows.

The boy has got some pie.
The mountains have got a lot of snow.

PAGE 42 ANSWERS TO THE WORKBOOK QUESTIONS **EXERCISE 1:**

1. *They've got a new house.*
2. *She's got a big family.*
3. *We've got some tea.*
4. *He's got a hamburger.*
5. *I've got a letter from my friend.*
6. *They've got a soccer ball.*
7. *We've got some English books.*
8. *The dog is happy. It's got a bone.*
9. *The students are busy. They've got work to do.*

PAGE 42 ANSWERS TO THE WORKBOOK QUESTIONS **EXERCISE 2:**

1. *He hasn't got a car.*
2. *The picture hasn't got many people.*
3. *Three of the men haven't got a bow.*
4. *They haven't got a soccer ball.*
5. *They haven't got any snow.*

Lesson 19 Continued

PAGE 43 ANSWERS TO THE WORKBOOK QUESTIONS **EXERCISE 3:**

1. They've got a new car.
2. Mexico City hasn't got any snow.
3. He's got to study.
4. They haven't got any money.
5. She's got to get her hair cut.
6. The dogs haven't got any home.
7. They haven't got any time to wait.
8. He's got something in his pocket.
9. The family hasn't got any food.
10. She's got a small house.

PAGE 43 ANSWERS TO THE WORKBOOK QUESTIONS **EXERCISE 4:**

1. The man in front *must* / *has to* / *has got to* pull.

2. Everyone *has to* / *must* / *has got to* help him.

3. The rope *must* not break.

4. They *must* / *have to* / *have got to* be strong.

5. They *have to* / *must* / *have got to* hold on to the rope.

PAGE 58 TEACHER'S GUIDE **ACTIVITY 4:**

Photocopy and cut the questions below into individual cards.
The students are to sit in two teams facing each other.
They are to take turns asking the students on the other team the questions.
Points may be given for correct answers.
Each student should ask and answer at least one question.

Lesson 19 Continued

Have you got a window in your house?
Yes, I've got a window in my house.

Have you got a bird in your house? *Yes, I've got a bird in my house.*
No, I haven't got a bird in my house.

Have you got a jacket?
Yes, I've got a jacket.
No, I haven't got a jacket.

Have you got a hat?
Yes, I've got a hat.
No, I haven't got a hat.

Have you got an elephant?
Yes, I've got an elephant.
No, I haven't got an elephant.

Have you got a book?
Yes, I've got a book.
No, I haven't got a book.

Have you got a watch?
Yes, I've got a watch.
No, I haven't got a watch.

Have you got a son?
Yes, I've got a son.
No, I haven't got a son.

Have you got two shoes?
Yes, I've got two shoes.

Have you got a pen?
Yes, I've got a pen.
No, I haven't got a pen.

Have you got a tie?
Yes, I've got a tie.
No, I haven't got a tie.

Have you got a door in your house?
Yes, I've got a door in my house.

Have you got a cat?
Yes, I've got a cat.
No, I haven't got a cat.

Have you got a ring?
Yes, I've got a ring.
No, I haven't got a ring.

Have you got a dog?
Yes, I've got a dog.
No, I haven't got a dog.

Have you got a daughter?
Yes, I've got a daughter.
No, I haven't got a daughter.

Lesson 20 Review

ORAL QUESTIONS

What time do you have breakfast?	I have breakfast at _____.
Is your friend older than you are?	Yes, my friend is older than I am.
	No, my friend isn't older than I am.
Which is better for you, juice or coffee?	_____ is better for me.
Are you interested in boats?	Yes, I'm interested in boats.
	No, I'm not interested in boats.
Did you get married yesterday?	Yes, I got married yesterday.
	No I didn't get married yesterday.
Who has the most books?	_____ has the most books.
Do you play basketball well?	Yes, I play basketball well.
	No, I don't play basketball well.
Do you eat quickly?	Yes, I eat quickly.
	No, I don't eat quickly.
Do you drive carefully?	Yes, I drive carefully.
	No, I don't drive carefully.
Do you ever go to town?	Yes, I go to town.
	No, I don't ever go to town.
Do you ever see your family?	Yes, I see my family.
	No, I don't ever see my family.
Have you got long dark hair?	Yes, I've got long dark hair.
	No, I haven't got long dark hair.
Did you ask for some juice?	Yes, I asked for some juice.
	No, I didn't ask for any juice.
Do you often wait for your friend?	Yes, I often wait for my friend.
	No, I don't often wait for my friend.
Are you often walking in the park?	Yes, I'm often walking in the park.
	No, I'm never walking in the park.
Do you usually buy bus tickets?	Yes, I usually buy bus tickets.
	No, I don't usually buy bus tickets.
Do you sometimes go swimming?	Yes, I sometimes go swimming.
	No, I never go swimming.
Who came to class the earliest?	_____ came to class the earliest.
Who came to class later than you did? Did you get time-off from work today?	_____ came to class later than I did. Yes, I got time-off from work today. No, I didn't get time-off from work today.
You ate breakfast this morning, didn't you?	Yes, I did. / No, I didn't.
You're in English class, aren't you?	Yes, I am.
You can't fly a plane, can you?	No, I can't. / Yes, I can.

Teacher Guide

Lesson 20 Continued

PAGE 44   ANSWERS TO THE WORKBOOK QUESTIONS   EXERCISE 1:

1. How far from the school do you live?
   I live _____ kilometers from the school.
2. Do you live farther from the school than Peter?
   Yes, I live farther from the school than Peter. / No, I don't live farther from the school…
3. Who lives the closest to the school, John, Jane, Miranda or Peter?
   John lives the closest to the school.
4. Does Jane live as near to the school as John?
   No, Jane doesn't live as near to the school as John.
5. Who lives the same distance from the school as Miranda?
   Jane lives the same distance from the school as Miranda.
6. Would you want to live as far from your school as Peter?
   Yes, I'd want to live as far from my school as Peter. / No, I wouldn't want to live as far…
7. Is the English School between Jane's house and Miranda's house?
   Yes, it's between Jane's house and Miranda's house.
   Yes, it's between their houses.

Note to the teacher:
Remind the students about the use of "ever". It isn't used in a positive sentence.

PAGE 45   ANSWERS TO THE WORKBOOK QUESTIONS   EXERCISE 2:

1. You came to English class today, *didn't you*?
   ANSWER: Yes, I did.
2. Canada is a big country, *isn't it*? **ANSWER: Yes, it is.**
3. You enjoy your holidays, *don't you*?
   ANSWER: Yes, I do.
4. You don't usually ride on an elephant, *do you*?
   ANSWER: No, I don't.
5. You aren't Canadian, *are you*?
   ANSWER: No, I'm not.
6. You can't fly, *can you*?
   ANSWER: No, I can't

PAGE 45   ANSWERS TO THE WORKBOOK QUESTIONS   EXERCISE 3:
Put these words into sentences.

1. *He has a big red car.*
2. *They liked the most expensive clothes in the store.*
3. *She wore a blue cotton dress.*
4. *Jim always rides his black bicycle.*
5. *Mary is usually late.*
6. *They will likely get married.*

PAGE 45   ANSWERS TO THE WORKBOOK QUESTIONS   EXERCISE 4:

Sarah and Peter were meeting their friends Tom and Carol. They'd waited *for / about* / fifteen minutes before the two friends finally arrived *at* the restaurant. Carol said that she'd slept *in* that morning and she was sorry. The four friends sat at a table across *from* each other and talked *about* the movie they saw last week.

They asked the waiter *for* some coffee. Then they all looked at the menu so they could decide what kind *of* dessert to order.

A JOKE: THE GOATS

The first goat answered: "The film was okay, but I liked the book better." If people read a book and then see a movie, they will often say that they liked the book better than the movie.
Because goats eat everything, the first goat is saying that the book tasted better than the film.

Teacher Guide

TEST 5   Lessons 1 TO 20

NAME _____ Answer these oral questions in sentences. (4 marks each)

1. _____
2. _____
3. _____
4. _____
5. _____
6. _____
7. _____
8. _____
9. _____
10. _____

Write these words in sentence order. (4 marks each)

11. beautiful, has, dress, a, red, She,

12. work, takes, bus, the, to, always, Jim

13. money, haven't, They, got, any

14. long, He, car, drove, a, black

15. late, is, usually, She

16. as, car, a, bicycle, fast, as, A, isn't

Teacher Guide   61

TEST 5 Continued

NAME: _____ **Answer in sentences: (4 marks each)**

17. Who lives the closest to Sarah's house?
_____

18. Who lives between Silvia and Sarah?
_____

19. Who lives the farthest from Tom's house?
_____

20. Who lives the same distance from Tom's house as Sarah?
_____

21. Who lives farther from the water than Tom?
_____

Use these words to complete the sentences. (2 marks each)

    at   for   up   in   about   from   for   in

Tom had to wait _____ Carol when he went to pick her _____ for English class. On the way there they talked _____ the movies they were the most interested _____. They arrived _____ class with the other students.

After class they went to a restaurant and asked the waiter _____ two hamburgers. They sat across _____ two other students who liked to play basketball. They talked about competing _____ many games with them.

ORAL QUESTIONS FOR TEST 5

ORAL QUESTIONS   ANSWERS (4 marks each)

1. Did you pick up your friend last night?

    Yes, I picked up my friend last night.
    No, I didn't pick up my friend last night.

2. Do you sometimes sleep in on Sundays?

    Yes, I sometimes sleep in on Sundays. No, I don't (never) sleep in on Sundays.

3. What day were you born?

    I was born on _____.

4. This is English class, isn't it?

    Yes, it is.

5. Is this the biggest city in the world?

    Yes, it's the biggest city in the world. No, it isn't the biggest city in the world.

6. Are you taller than your friend (is)?

    Yes, I'm taller than my friend (is)
    No, I'm not taller than my friend (is).

7. Do you buy the most expensive clothes?

    Yes, I buy the most expensive clothes. No, I don't buy the most expensive clothes.

8. Is this the worst time of year?

    Yes, it's / this is the worst time of year. No, it / this isn't the worst time of year. It's the best time of year.

9. Do you ever go to town?

    Yes, I go to town.
    No, I don't ever go to town.

10. Have you got a dog?

    Yes, I've got a dog.
    No, I haven't got a dog.

ANSWERS TO TEST 5 QUESTIONS

Write these words in sentence order. (4 marks each)

11. beautiful, has, dress, a, red, She, *She has a beautiful red dress.*
12. work, takes, bus, the, to, always, Jim *Jim always takes the bus to work.*
13. money, haven't, They, got, any *They haven't got any money.*
14. long, He, car, drove, a, black *He drove a long black car.*
15. late, is, usually, She *She is usually late.*
16. as, car, a, bicycle, fast, as, A, isn't *A bicycle isn't as fast as a car.*

Teacher Guide

Answers to Test 5 Continued

Answer in sentences: (4 marks each)

17. Who lives the closest to Sarah's house?
    Tom lives the closest to Sarah's house. 18.
    Who lives between Silvia and Sarah?
    Tom lives between Silvia and Sarah.

19. Who lives the farthest from Tom's house?
    John lives the farthest from Tom's house.

20. Who lives the same distance from Tom's house as Sarah?
    Silvia lives the same distance from Tom's house as Sarah.
21. Who lives farther from the water than Tom?
    Sarah lives farther from the water than Tom.

Use these words to complete the sentences. (2 marks each)
at   for   up   in   about from   for   in

Tom had to wait **_for_** Carol when he went to pick her **_up_** for English class. On the way there they talked **_about_** the movies they were the most interested **_in_**. They arrived **_at_** / **_in_** / **_for_** class with the other students.

After class they went to a restaurant and asked the waiter **_for_** two hamburgers. They sat across **_from_** two other students who liked to play basketball. They talked about competing **_in_** many games with them.

Visit us Online for More

https://www.efl-esl.com

BEGINNERS ESL LESSON PLANS BOOK 1

BEGINNERS LESSON PLANS BOOK 1

**20 complete lesson plans
3 Textbooks plus
Downloadable Audio and Video**

Includes:

- Student Reader
- Student Workbook
- Teachers Guide
- 20 lessons
- 5 tests
- 4 reviews
- Glossary
- Download PDF or Paperback

Book 1 Overview

BEGINNERS ESL LESSON PLANS BOOK 2

BEGINNERS LESSON PLANS BOOK 2

**20 complete lesson plans
3 Textbooks plus
Downloadable Audio and Video**

Includes:

- Student Reader
- Student Workbook
- Teachers Guide
- 20 lessons
- 5 tests
- 4 reviews
- Glossary
- Download PDF or Paperback

Book 2 Overview

Listening and Speaking Workbook

Complete Listening and Speaking English Workbook – includes full downloadable audio!

- Vocabulary for each Lesson
- Everyday Conversations – Listen to full audio then role-play!
- 14 Lessons
- 2 Review Chapters
- 2 Full Audio Tests with Answer Key
- Role Play
- Telephone Conversations and role play
- Question and Answer Dialogues

https://efl-esl.com/listening-speaking-english/

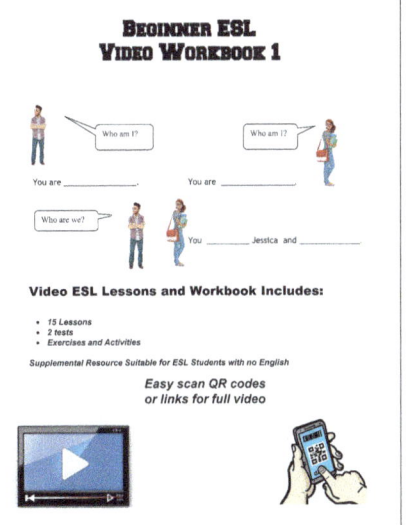

Beginners ESL Video Workbook

Includes:

- 15 lesson plans with full video
- Supplemental activities and games
- Video introduction for all topics

Learn More https://efl-esl.com/video-workbooks/

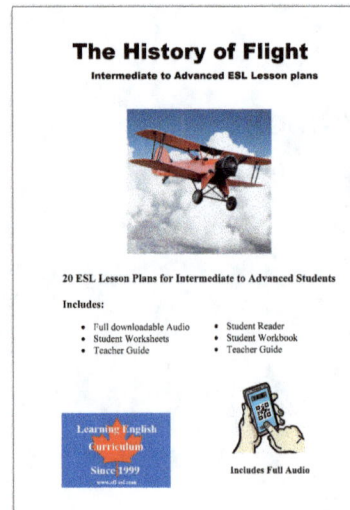

Intermediate to Advanced ESL Lesson Plans for Adults
From the Ancient Greeks to Leonardo Da Vinci's flying machines, to Orville and Wilbur Wright, to WWII flying Ace, the Red Baron, to modern day space travel!

Includes:

- **Full audio**
- 20 Lessons – 40 hours of classroom time!
- Print as many Copies as Required!
- Teacher's guide
- Student Reader
- Student Workbook
- Complete instructions — ready for the classroom
- No preparation

https://efl-esl.com/curriculum/flight/

Children's ESL

This book introduces the alphabet from A to L and the numbers from 1 – 10.

Includes:

- Student book – 37 pages
- Student Workbook – 24 pages
- Teacher's Guide Book – 50 pages
- Glossary — 142 new words
- Colorful games and activities suitable for lamination –use over and over!

https://efl-esl.com/alphabet-activities-for-esl-students/

ESL Graphic Novels for Kids (Comic Books)

These books offer an oral approach for young ESL / EFL students aged 6 - 10.

They contain high interest stories, written in the graphics novel format that children love. This is very suitable for supplementary study, home school, as well as for summer camps.

https://efl-esl.com/esl-graphic-novels-for-children/

www.ingramcontent.com/pod-product-compliance
Lightning Source LLC
LaVergne TN
LVHW080249260326
834688LV00042BA/1194